The BRILLIANCE in FAILURE

Nik Acharya,

I am so glad you enjoyed the book. It was so much fun to write.

Hopefully you will get the chance to share your leadership journey someday -

The BRILLIANCE in FAILURE

A Leader's Learning Journey

CHRISTIAN A. BRICKMAN

ARCHWAY PUBLISHING

Copyright © 2014 Christian A. Brickman.

All rights reserved. No part of this book may be used or reproduced by any means, graphic, electronic, or mechanical, including photocopying, recording, taping or by any information storage retrieval system without the written permission of the publisher except in the case of brief quotations embodied in critical articles and reviews.

Archway Publishing books may be ordered through booksellers or by contacting:

Archway Publishing
1663 Liberty Drive
Bloomington, IN 47403
www.archwaypublishing.com
1-(888)-242-5904

Because of the dynamic nature of the Internet, any web addresses or links contained in this book may have changed since publication and may no longer be valid. The views expressed in this work are solely those of the author and do not necessarily reflect the views of the publisher, and the publisher hereby disclaims any responsibility for them.

Any people depicted in stock imagery provided by Thinkstock are models, and such images are being used for illustrative purposes only. Certain stock imagery © Thinkstock.

ISBN: 978-1-4808-1197-3 (sc)
ISBN: 978-1-4808-1196-6 (hc)
ISBN: 978-1-4808-1203-1 (e)

Library of Congress Control Number: 2014917776

Printed in the United States of America.

Archway Publishing rev. date: 10/29/2014

To my wife, Cindy, who has walked every step of the journey with me, and to my dog, Eddie, who somehow manages to greet every person he meets with kindness and joy.

I would like to acknowledge all of the leaders who believed in and invested in me.

CONTENTS

Chapter 1	Fail Fast, Learn Faster	xi
Chapter 2	On the Wrong Foot	1
Chapter 3	Failure Isn't Fatal	12
Chapter 4	Release Your Agenda	21
Chapter 5	Drop the Baggage	31
Chapter 6	Listen for the Gold	41
Chapter 7	Humility and the Art of Asking for Help	51
Chapter 8	The Cruel Joke	61
Chapter 9	Never Burn Bridges	70
Chapter 10	The 80/20 Rule	80
Chapter 11	Transparency Changes Everything	90
Chapter 12	On Greed and Gravitas	100
Chapter 13	The Do-Nothing Strategy	110
Chapter 14	The Why Always Comes Before the What	121
Chapter 15	The Toughest Calls Are the Most Important	130
Chapter 16	The Worst Part of the Job	139
Chapter 17	Be a Coach, Not a Critic	148

Chapter 18	Sharing the Stage......................................157
Chapter 19	Piercing the Bubble 166
Chapter 20	An Evolving Lens.......................................174

INTRODUCTION

Fail Fast, Learn Faster

The hypothesis I would ask you to consider as you begin this book is very simple: you are not perfect, the people you work with are not perfect, and the company you work for is not perfect. The implication of all this imperfection is that failure is almost inevitable. It is not something to be feared or avoided. It is simply part of life, and it will be part of your career as well.

The inevitability of failure is not an easy thing for high-performing people to accept because they typically grow up succeeding at everything they do. It is easy for people like this to get accustomed to being at the top of the class, whether in college, in the first job, in business school, or as they scale the corporate ladder. Success can become addictive, and failure is anathema. But long-term success does not come without a healthy dose of failure mixed in.

As a result, sustainable success is likely to be determined by how you react to failure and how quickly you learn from it, regardless of the disappointment or regret you may feel about failing at something. So, accept the fact that failure will find you, no matter how talented or lucky you are. I cannot tell you today what form that failure will take, but it will happen, and it will happen multiple times throughout your career.

Failure has found me many times. Most of the time, the setbacks I endured were self-inflicted. I had a lot of growing up to do as a young leader, which led to a plethora of mistakes and plenty of learning. But setbacks and challenges will come from external sources as well. The market for your product or service may dry up; competitors may innovate and steal share; or macroeconomic conditions might deteriorate on a wide scale. Whatever the driver of the failure, it is likely that you will be thrown a few external curveballs during the course of your career.

Given all of the likely setbacks and challenges that are lurking in the future, learning how to take all of this in stride, including learning from the experience and then moving onward and upward, is a key skill or capability that every leader will have to build. I have worked for eight different companies and held thirteen different jobs over a twenty-eight-year career. I have known both great success and great failure over that time, and I have survived both. However, I am not going to talk much about the successes.

My goal in writing this book is to share many of the failures and mistakes I have made during my career, in order to highlight the learning and development opportunities those failures created for me.

The insights and learnings I have gained from these experiences have shaped my leadership style and ground the lens through which I view and evaluate leaders today. I do not regret the fact that I have made mistakes and failed in some circumstances. I relish those experiences because I have learned so much and they made me a much better leader over time. That is my hope for you as well—that you can learn from my mistakes and experiences, as well as your own, and become a better leader.

Leadership is not a static event. It is a learning journey that will last your entire career and life. In fact, I think the learning can actually accelerate as you become more senior and more advanced in your career because you are more open to it. By that I mean that you become more confident in yourself and the value you bring, as well as more accepting of your blind spots and the opportunities to continue growing as a leader.

My learning journey continues to unfold before me. Despite the mistakes I have made and the setbacks I have faced, I have managed to stay focused on learning from those experiences and moving forward in my career.

That commitment to continuous learning has taken me to the top echelon of corporate leadership, but more importantly, it has helped me become a better coach and mentor for other leaders who also have the energy and courage to learn from their mistakes and keep moving forward on their leadership careers. And that is the best reward in the end—the opportunity to help others find the path to success and unlock their potential, no matter what challenges they might confront in the process.

To maintain continuity of thought throughout the following chapters, in which the ideas and examples I present may not be in chronological order, I'd like to simply list the companies for which I have worked in the correct order of my career path: The Boston Consulting Group, The NutraSweet Company, CSC Index Consulting, Guinness/United Distillers LTD, Whitlock Packaging Corporation, McKinsey & Co., Kimberly-Clark Corporation, and Sally Beauty Holdings, Inc.

CHAPTER 1

On the Wrong Foot

The insecurities and personal issues we develop during childhood often follow us into our adult lives, and they have a surprising ability to diminish our impact and undermine our potential. When I started my first job, I was desperately insecure, but I was also an expert at covering it up with bravado and cockiness. I had grown up as the second child of a demanding family, and I was desperate to prove myself and stand out.

Throughout much of my early life, I felt like the extra wheel in the family; I did not play a musical instrument, at least not well, but my brother did. I was not as well-read as the rest of the family, and it showed. I was competitive in sports, but never an exceptional athlete. I did well in school, but I was not at the top of my class. I did well on the SATs, but not as well as my brother. I went to a good college, but not a great one. Everything was fine, but nothing was exceptional, and that was a hard thing to accept in an achievement-oriented family.

As I finished college, I was starting to find my stride and achieve results consistent with my potential. I was intensely competitive, which motivated me to work hard and strive for more. But the damage had been done in terms of the character imperfections I would carry with me during my early career.

I was prone to making arrogant statements to draw attention to myself. I would repeat things I should have kept confidential because I thought that would make people see me as "in the know." I would often embellish the facts to make my stories sound better. And I had a really hard time listening. I was always focused on figuring out the best response, rather than genuinely learning from the person I was talking to. I was smart and energetic, but I was laden with imperfections that had a huge impact on my early career.

As I look back now, I am surprised I never got fired, especially given the demanding places I worked during those early years. Lucky for me, I had some strong underlying skills, and I found a few sponsors who were willing to look beyond the façade. However, I had to learn some difficult lessons during my first five to seven years of work experience.

My career began at an elite consulting firm in Chicago, but the learning experiences started while I was still in school at Occidental College. During the fall of my senior year, I decided to interview at various companies in an attempt to hone my interview skills and understand the options that were available to new graduates.

I interviewed with a number of large companies, two consulting firms, and an investment bank. I found that I was pretty good at the process. I had a solid academic and extracurricular history; I was enthusiastic and inquisitive; and I was able to cover up the fact that I knew absolutely nothing about business other than it seemed like the best place to find a job.

As luck would have it, The Boston Consulting Group had decided to interview on my campus that year because the person recruiting for the Chicago office was an Occidental College graduate. I submitted my credentials and was selected to interview. Consulting firms like BCG use the case method of interviewing, in which they challenge candidates with business cases to test their problem-solving skills. Some of the other candidates found the case method intimidating, but I loved it. Problem-solving real business situations was much more engaging than talking about my resume over and over again.

After the first round of interviews on campus, I was called back to a final round of interviews in Chicago. It was an overwhelming experience: BCG sent me an airline ticket, put me up in a suite at the Ritz Carlton Chicago—which was by far the finest hotel I had ever stayed in—and took me out to a fabulous dinner after a full day of interviews.

One thing that I remember vividly is that Chicago was really cold that day, and I was completely unprepared for the weather. I had no long underwear, so underneath my suit, I wore the leopard spandex tights that I had used in an air band contest the weekend before. I pulled my socks up as high as possible that morning, before my second round of interviews, so that nobody would notice the leopard-print fabric on my lower legs.

On the way to the office from the hotel, I realized that I did not have enough money for cab fare, so I had to jump out of the cab six blocks short of my destination and walk the rest of the way in fifteen-degree weather and a light snow, with no overcoat. Despite that setback, I still made it to the BCG office on time and ready for the full day of interviews.

I remember almost nothing else about that day. It was fast-paced, intense, and exhausting. But by the end of the day, I had an offer in hand for a base annual salary of $30,000, with a bonus of up to $6,000, based on performance. That amount seemed like an awful lot of money to a college student in 1986. I learned later that money goes fast in a big city like Chicago. But when I received the offer, it was an exciting and proud moment. I saw the chance to start my career at an incredible company that worked on challenging client issues and had a reputation for hiring incredibly talented people. But I quickly began to undermine myself.

At dinner that night with the second-year analysts, I bragged about my offer and salary, which was a big issue, because the firm had raised the salary for first-year analysts, but had yet to tell the previous year's class or adjust their compensation accordingly.

When I got back to school, I learned that the recruiting director had considered rescinding my offer as a result of that indiscretion. Luckily for me, he decided not to do that. But that experience did not slow me down. I bragged about my offer to everyone who would listen, and I think I alienated half of my senior classmates in the process.

That type of behavior continued throughout most of my early work experience. I would make inappropriate statements to draw attention to myself; I would share information I should have held in confidence; I would slightly alter the facts to make stories and information sound better. All of these tactics were intended to draw attention to myself or to get other people to like me or think better of me. I am sure that my behavior came off as arrogant and cocky to most people, but it was really the opposite. I had deep insecurities left over from my formative years, and these compensating behaviors were designed to cover up that fact.

I was burned a number of times in my career by these undermining behaviors. I remember very specific situations where I told a little white lie to make a story sound better, but then I would have to tell additional lies in order to maintain the first one. I also remember sharing confidential information with a coworker, and then I remember spending weeks worrying and agonizing over whether that information would be shared again—and somehow the breach of confidence would get back to me. I made my own life miserable at times, and I am sure I compromised the confidence and trust of the people I worked with. It was stupid and self-defeating, but it was who I was at that point in my life and career.

Today, as a senior executive, I see these same traits in young executives all the time. I call it wrestling with the demons, and I laugh a bit at the old me every time I work with a young leader who is making the same mistakes that I did early in my career. I empathize with them—everybody has a few demons and imperfections they carry from early life, and these affect their behavior and relationships in the work environment. These demons vary in terms of their severity and duration, but they affect most people, and learning to manage and mitigate them is part of the maturation and development process.

Honestly, the first step in wrestling these demons to the ground is simply awareness. It is easy to recognize these issues and behaviors later in life, with the benefit of experience, but most of us are simply not very self-aware early in our lives. I certainly was not. In fact, some people never seem to achieve true self-awareness.

The reality we have to come to terms with is simply that we are not perfect, and nobody expects us to be perfect. Humans are fundamentally flawed, and each of us brings our own set of imperfections and demons. But we can learn. If we are open to it, we can gather feedback from people we trust, learn from that, try to incorporate the feedback into our daily interactions, and grow as leaders and people.

Unfortunately, I learned most of my lessons the hard way. I failed to recognize how I was letting my own insecurities affect me in the moment. As a result, I made lots of mistakes and bad choices. I learned by having near career-ending experiences early. It took a while, but it was effective over time.

Later in life, I discovered that owning up to my imperfections goes a long way toward building trust with my team and colleagues. I regularly write e-mails to share ideas and insights with my teams. The following is the content of an e-mail to my direct reports that I sent when I was president of the International Division of Kimberly-Clark. My goal was to present some of the imperfections and flaws that I struggled with as a leader so my colleagues could understand and relate to me better. I hoped it would enable them to feel comfortable giving me feedback if they observed some of these behaviors in me. I was really surprised by the responses I received.

> Subject: True North—the leadership edition
>
> Perfection is a myth. We can pursue it, aspire to it, and desire it, but we will never achieve it. Despite this

fact, we are often driven by the myth of perfection, and we agonize over our failures, mistakes, and shortcomings. I have witnessed very capable leaders worry that their issues or development areas would be perceived as serious weaknesses that might undermine their career paths.

As a result, they sometimes went to great lengths to hide or cover them up, which was futile because we all saw them, and the cover-up just looked silly (or worse—dishonest). It is ironic that their attempts to be perfect actually diminished their impact as leaders.

I know that I felt this way as a young leader, and it drove some terrible leadership behavior on my part. I wanted so badly to show that I could be the perfect leader that I sometimes failed to be straightforward, direct, and honest with my teams. As a result, I undermined their trust in me.

What I have learned over time is that people value transparency and honesty much more than they value perfection, recognizing that it is a myth. I had to get comfortable with who I was, what I was good at, and what my weaknesses were before I could aspire to being a good leader. I had to be honest with myself and my teams about a few things:

1) That I still agonize over results and performance. I got this from my mom, who was incredibly demanding of herself and her kids. My upbringing makes me prone to launching too many ideas and initiatives because I so desperately want to improve and win. I have to work at staying focused on the big ideas and ask others to challenge me if I am distracting the team. I fight this every single day I come to work.

2) That I talk too much and do not listen enough. I grew up in a family where I had to fight for air time among some very smart people, and I am still fighting that battle. Some might argue I am still losing that battle. Because of this, I have to practice asking more questions and giving people more time to respond. It does not come easily, so I am still working hard on this one.

3) That I tend to over-react in the moment. I am a high-energy person, and when I get really worked up about something I want to attack it (or them). I must practice the twenty-four-hour rule a mentor once asked me to try out. He simply asked me to wait twenty-four hours before responding, and if I still felt the same way after a day, fine, but typically, I find that I have a cooler head the next day. I apply this rule during the most difficult and challenging moments, and when I stick to it, I find I respond in a very balanced way. When I do not apply the rule, I am often disappointed with myself later.

4) That I jump to the answer too quickly sometimes. I am very impatient, and I want to get to a decision or an action so badly that I skip over the details. I need people on my team who will dig deeper and ask tough questions that I might overlook. And I need to block time on my calendar to dig through the numbers to make sure I am grounded in a reasonable level of rigor.

These are just a few of my imperfections. The point is that we are all imperfect; we are all works in progress. That does not mean we cannot be great leaders; it simply means we have to work at it. The moment you can be completely transparent about your weaknesses with the people around you is the very moment you will find your "true north" as a leader. When you lay yourself bare and allow your teams inside, they will truly trust you and want to follow you.

If you want to achieve your full potential as a leader, to find your "true north," start by being completely honest and transparent with yourself and the people around you. Admit to every weakness and reveal battle scars. Make those imperfections part of your becoming better, because they will elevate your game if you let them.
Chris

The e-mail with that content went somewhat viral inside Kimberly-Clark, and I received dozens of e-mails, from people across the company, thanking me for being so transparent and open as a senior leader. I did not think much of it at the time, but I realize now that sharing these imperfections probably made me more human and approachable to people who often see senior executives as arrogant and distant.

Being honest about who I was, and what my demons were, allowed people to relate to me personally because I wrestled with the same issues and challenges as everyone else. It is somewhat ironic that I spent the first part of my career trying to cover up my insecurities and imperfections, only to discover later in my career that being openly imperfect actually made people feel better about me as a person and more trusting of me as a leader.

Over time, I have discovered that the ability of leaders to see themselves as they really are, as others see them—to honestly assess their strengths, their weaknesses, and their demons—is game changing. Self-awareness unlocks everything. It allows them to build teams that mitigate their weaknesses, to recognize situations that might trigger old feelings and insecurities, and to take a deep breath before responding in the moment.

Self-awareness enables leaders to open up the strategic discussion or dialogue with the leadership teams, to explore a broader range of options, and to be open and honest with their teams and colleagues in a way that builds genuine trust and transparency. Self-awareness can fundamentally change the impact a leader can have on an organization.

Unlocking this potential is what I focus on in development discussions with leaders today. I find that the right coaching and friendly feedback can make a significant impact if delivered well. I have to wonder about senior executives who show no empathy for young leaders still struggling with their demons, as if they themselves had no development challenges and needs as young leaders.

I have observed senior leaders criticizing talented young executives who are still learning to manage and mitigate their demons. Those leaders can be quick to dismiss the younger executives' skills, but they are missing the real opportunity when they act this way.

The breakthrough opportunity is to find a way to wrap our arms around those leaders and provide them with the coaching and mentorship they need to overcome their personal issues and challenges.

The objective should not be to judge them, but rather to build a better team and a deeper talent bench over time. Accomplishing that goal is not just about being tough and demanding in the performance dialogue. It is also about helping young leaders confront their demons and recognize their self-defeating behaviors so that they can reach their full potential. Sometimes there are exceptionally talented leaders buried behind a façade of demons they have yet to wrestle to the ground. I try my best to look for and unlock that possibility.

CHAPTER 2

Failure Isn't Fatal

I left Boston Consulting Group in 1989 and joined the NutraSweet Company as manager of strategy and capital analysis. At that time, NutraSweet was a very profitable division of Monsanto, which held the patent for Aspartame, the artificial sweetener that is still used in most diet soft drinks today. I was hired by a former BCG colleague who had recently been appointed the VP of finance for the largest division of NutraSweet. He was one of those long-term mentors able to see past the imperfections and recognize potential in me.

When I joined the company early that summer, I was twenty-four years old. I was full of ideas and energy, but I lacked any semblance of corporate decorum, style, or gravitas. However, NutraSweet was a good company for me to jump to. It was small in absolute size; it had grown up very fast, so it lacked much process or structure; and it was a free-flowing environment, where a young leader could work on important issues and get substantial exposure to senior leadership.

During my first couple of years there, I really enjoyed the experience. I worked on the contract and price negotiations with our major customers, helped the senior team think through our strategy relative to the alternative sugar substitutes that were being developed by our competitors, had the opportunity to work extensively on our European business, and traveled abroad frequently. Additionally, I worked on evaluating a number of large capital projects and strategic investments that the company was considering.

The leadership team was surprisingly tolerant of my immaturity, and they valued the strategic analysis skills I had learned during my two and a half years at BCG. It was an exciting experience, and I was regularly included in strategic discussions with the CEO and the top team.

I also had the opportunity to build a strategy team that focused on completing the detailed analysis required to make sure those discussions were rigorous. My small, but capable, team got to sit through (and even participate in) some very strategic negotiation sessions with our largest customers and observe some real experts at negotiation in action. It was definitely a great developmental experience for all of us.

But things started to change somewhere around the two-year mark. A new CEO was brought in from another Monsanto division who was a little more "old school," and he had a hard time accepting twenty-six-year-old leaders at the decision-making table. In addition, the company went through a restructuring, and the mentor who had originally brought me to NutraSweet left the company. Finally, the division president who had leveraged my skills in strategic analysis and negotiations moved on to a new position, and his replacement had a much more formal style.

All of this caused me to question my position at

the company, and I wondered whether this new set of leaders would be as supportive of my development. As a result, I started looking outside the company for a new opportunity. I updated my resume and began to connect with search firms, which were unlikely to have noticed my career up to that point.

I also reconnected with friends at BCG to get their guidance. To my surprise, one of those former colleagues suggested that I should interview for a consultant position at the firm (the role into which they hire MBAs), indicating that the firm might be willing to consider my corporate experience as roughly equivalent to an MBA. He helped me enter the recruiting process at BCG, and on my own, I was able to initiate the process with another well-regarded firm, A. T. Kearney.

As a result, I was feeling pretty confident that one of the two firms would make me an offer and that this would help me maintain and accelerate my career trajectory. I thought this would help address the concern raised by some search executives about my lack of an MBA, especially when compared with other high-potential candidates.

I do not remember the specifics of the recruiting process, but both firms put me through a significant number of interviews that included a mixture of case studies and more traditional interviews. I also recall that the process dragged out over a couple of weeks and multiple rounds, but I got callbacks each time, and my confidence grew that an offer was forthcoming.

It was at this point in the process that I let my confidence, or arrogance, and my frustration over the situation at NutraSweet, get the best of me. I began to brag about the great opportunity I foresaw to go back into consulting, how much money I was going to make, and how I was done with NutraSweet. Within a few days, I managed to share my plans with much of the senior staff, and it was broadly known within the company that I was planning to leave. It was completely unnecessary, it was stupid, and it turned out to be a huge mistake.

The next week I heard from both firms. Although the details are somewhat fuzzy after more than two decades, I remember that I heard from A. T. Kearney first: apparently one partner there felt I was overconfident and arrogant, and they had decided not to proceed further. It was disappointing, because I had heard directly from a few people at the firm who were very supportive, but I still had the BCG opportunity on the hook, and that was my preferred firm.

I remember receiving the call from BCG on a Friday afternoon. As soon as the conversation began, I knew I was in trouble. I had been confident that they were going to extend an offer, but the answer was something like, "we have decided not to proceed." It was devastating. I was twenty-six years old, newly married, with a new house and mortgage, and I had shot myself in the foot with my current employer before I had learned the final outcome with my new opportunities. *How could I have been that stupid? What was I going to do now?*

The disappointment and regret I felt made for a very long weekend. I was not sure what to do. I could go into work Monday and "eat crow," but I was not sure that was going to save my job, and no other job opportunities were even close. It was early 1991, and the job environment was not particularly robust. I remember agonizing over my predicament for most of the weekend—and being too embarrassed to share the full gravity of the situation with my new wife.

I felt as if everything I had worked for thus far in my career was in jeopardy, and I was physically sick to my stomach. Additionally, I developed a red rash on the inside of my arms, which was completely stress-related. My wife has now learned to look for this rash as a sign of how much stress I am undergoing.

Finally, late Sunday night as I tossed in bed, I made up my mind about how I was going to turn the situation around. I knew that NutraSweet faced a huge day of reckoning with a patent expiration, which was coming in less than two years. I knew that I had developed a deep understanding of our pricing strategy, our customer and competitive situations, and the likely cost and attractiveness of alternative sweeteners. I also knew the economics of potential entrants that might be considering Aspartame capacity investments.

My plan was simple: I was going to work my tail off to bring all of this together into a cohesive post-patent pricing and negotiation strategy and engage all of the key stakeholders in the company to help frame it. I was going to focus on being a totally committed leader of that essential strategy and deflect any conversation about my potential departure.

The following week, I began to do just that. I pulled together all of the pricing data for each customer (and for every country in the world). I laid out a range of pricing scenarios on a customer and consolidated basis, along with likely competitive entry scenarios, and I assessed the potential "profit at risk" under each scenario. Then I made appointments and presented that strategic analysis to all of the key stakeholders in the company.

Occasionally, a leader would end the hour of discussing the work by saying, "I thought you were leaving." I tried to answer that in a genuinely humble way by admitting to the mistake I had made but then quickly focusing on how excited I was about executing the post-patent strategy and how I could add value to the process.

I pushed on this analysis for two very intense weeks, working long hours and trying to incorporate the feedback of all of the leaders with whom I met. I had to admit my stupid mistake to at least ten people, but the noise was quickly fading, and I was getting a lot of positive feedback on the work and how it was helping clarify our go-forward strategy at an important time for the company.

After about three weeks of intense effort and real progress, I found myself sharing an elevator ride with the new division president. We had not talked much, and this moment was no different, but at some point in the awkward silence, he turned to me and said something to the effect of, "I thought you were leaving." He then got off the elevator and went to his office. His comment felt like a kick in the stomach, but I knew I deserved it, so rather than skulk back in my office, I booked an appointment on his calendar the following day and prepared to "eat crow" one more time.

A day later, I was sitting in his office looking across his imposing desk. I started by referencing the comment he had made the day before, and I admitted that I deserved it. I talked about how I had made an immature mistake that I regretted deeply. Then I turned the conversation to the value I thought I could add to the company. I explained how I was aligning the team around a clear post-patent strategy and investing the time to build real rigor around that strategy. Finally, I ended with a clear commitment to helping the team navigate the daunting process of patent expiration that was fast approaching.

I then took a deep breath and waited for his response. I do not remember his exact words, but I remember the following:
- He thanked me for having the courage to come to his office, admit my mistake, and take responsibility for my actions.
- He coached me on how I should be more thoughtful and mature going forward.
- And then he told me he was glad to have me on the team and to focus on driving the strategy and helping the team develop and execute the post-patent plan.

As I walked back to my office, I had a huge smile on my face. In the course of just three weeks, I had gone from being devastated and almost unemployed to being a key member of the leadership team. I had shot myself in the foot through my own arrogance and immaturity, but I had recovered and invested myself completely in work that made a difference to the company, and I had managed to lift myself back up off the ground and hit the reset button.

I went home that night and slept really well for the first time in three weeks. Ultimately, I stayed almost two more years at NutraSweet, and I had a great time helping all of our customer teams secure long-term post-patent contracts, which were key to ensuring the profitability of the company through patent expiration.

All of us make mistakes in our career, some bigger than

others. It is just part of life. We will fail at times; we will do things that will later cause us to look back and wonder, *what was I thinking?* It is a natural part of life to experience twists and turns in the course of our careers. The real question is not whether a leader will get knocked down—everyone will. It is whether (and how quickly) he or she can get back up. In my case, my own arrogance knocked me off my feet, but with a little tenacity and focus, I was able to get back in the game and head in a positive direction.

As a senior executive, I have watched leaders face huge setbacks in their lives and careers but still find a way to pick themselves up and refocus their energy. Their ability to cope with failure and see it as merely "delayed success" is inspiring. To be successful, I think companies need more of these people. So many companies seem paralyzed by the fear of failure, they over-analyze every decision in the hope of finding the perfect answer, but in the process, they slow down decision-making, and they seem to kill every bold idea that involves even a modicum of risk.

Courageous leaders who have overcome failure in their lives change this dynamic—they reframe it. They push the team forward and force the people around them to learn from the experience and try again. Most important, when the worst of times come, they do not freeze. They bring the team together, focus the conversation and the problem-solving agenda, and they take action. They lean forward in the face of headwinds, and they refuse to accept failure as the outcome.

This is the central learning from my experience: It is easy to get paralyzed when failure happens. That paralysis leads some people to shut down and retrench. But successful people fundamentally reject that option.

They get back up, and they dig back in—no matter how embarrassed they might be about the mistakes they have made. The best people I have worked with over time have all failed—that is not the issue—but in each case, they refocused their energy on something they were passionate about and managed to deliver their best and most creative work exactly when they needed it most.

I would hire a leader who has suffered substantial setbacks and overcome them over a leader who has only known success, any day. The leader who has failed and recovered will not panic or wilt in the face of adversity. A tested leader will maintain calm and focus, helping the team regroup, reframe, and refocus.

Do not fear failure, but rather embrace it, take responsibility for it, and learn from it. And then refocus on finding a new path to success. The quicker you step up and take ownership for a mistake, the sooner you can begin to fix it, and the more people will respect you for acting in an accountable way. It will take energy and resilience, but if you can push yourself to rebound and move forward, you can unlock new possibilities for yourself and those around you. More important, you will develop a mental toughness that will leave you better prepared for the next challenge or failure, which will inevitably come.

CHAPTER 3

Release Your Agenda

We all have agendas. An agenda could consist of definitive plans or desired outcomes we are working toward. It could simply be our initial opinions regarding the best answers or approaches to problems. Whatever the case, when we walk into a room to engage in a problem-solving dialogue with a team, we bring our agendas with us, and that affects how much we listen, to whom we listen, and how open we are to the insights and ideas of others.

As I have grown in my career, I have learned that I have to force myself to release my agenda, so that I can listen to and incorporate the great ideas of the team. This does not mean that I do not have a clear opinion; it simply means that I try to frame the priorities and then open the floor for debate.

I have to encourage people to challenge my thinking and make it better. It is something that takes practice because it can feel like the decision-making process is actually slowing down. However, it is worth the effort, as it can make the final agenda better and drive alignment and ownership within the team. But for someone as impatient and action-oriented as I am, this approach requires focus and commitment, as well as a touch of patience.

As a young executive, I struggled with this issue. I can remember many great examples throughout my career, but one that sticks out happened during a client engagement with a large alcoholic-beverage company. I had left NutraSweet to take an engagement manager role at CSC Index, an upstart consulting firm that was growing rapidly based on the hot concept of reengineering. I joined the firm in the spring of 1993. Initially, I focused on helping the company build an analyst program, in order to augment the analytical rigor they brought to their client engagements.

After about six months, I began developing and serving clients. One of the first projects was focused on helping a huge beverage company radically rethink its distribution/go-to-market model. It was a "clean slate" project, where the client team was located offsite and chartered to think outside the norm in terms of the final approach or answer.

It was a challenging project for a very large and proud company, but it was also an exciting business issue and a fun client team. The location, in a loft building situated in a waterfront bar and nightclub area, made it even more exciting for the team. We worked in close quarters with the client team, with the goal of clean-slating the entire GTM model and developing a long-term vision of how the network should evolve over time.

Once we had established the future-state vision, the plan was to develop a set of specific action steps that the company could take to begin transforming the current model. Overall, the team dynamic was positive, and the CSC Index team worked closely with the client team to develop the future-state vision.

But as the final deadline for the project approached, we

struggled to get alignment across the team. The specific areas of disagreement are unclear to me today, but I remember that we scheduled a series of working sessions with the entire client team to work through the proposal and edit the final presentation, which would capture the recommendations that we would make to the senior leadership.

I also remember my mindset going into these workshops: I was confident that we had the right answer and that we had tested it sufficiently through interviews and analysis. The work had been widely shared with senior leadership at the company in advance to test for alignment. As a result, I went into these workshops with the goal of convincing the dissenting client team members, who still disagreed with our current answer, that my way was the best way. I was not thinking about how to listen to their ideas and incorporate them into the design. I was focused on finishing the work and the presentation as quickly as possible.

On one of the final afternoons, we ended up in a heated debate, which went on late into the evening. I continued to argue the merits and logic of the future-state design around which most of the team had aligned. I was pretty good at debating and arguing my opinion, but other members of the team continued to argue for their perspective, and we made absolutely no progress toward finalizing the design recommendation or the presentation.

The harder I pushed and argued for one answer, the more entrenched the other side seemed to become—and the more angry. In the end, I think I wore them down, and we decided to call it a night and go forward with the recommendation as it stood. But it was clear that there was lingering resentment and a lack of real alignment with the full client team.

As I look back on that experience today, I understand why I failed to get genuine alignment and buy-in. I was not listening to the alternative insights and perspectives with the goal of learning from them. I was focused on refuting their data and convincing them they were wrong, which is a fundamentally flawed approach because no one wants to be convinced that they are wrong.

If I had been willing to release my agenda and simply say, "I understand your concern. Tell me how we could incorporate something into the design that would address that." Alternatively, if I had asked them to come up and take the pen for a moment to show the team how we might incorporate their ideas into the design in order to improve the final output, I could have completely changed the dynamic in that room.

I could have challenged and empowered the client team to find a solution that addressed the legitimate concerns they were raising. By taking some time to listen to them and help them get their ideas on the table and included, I could have helped the team align around the proposal and the next steps much faster.

Over the years, I have struggled to develop the open-mindedness required to allow other ideas to affect my initial thoughts. It is easy for me to fall back on old habits, wherein I quickly make up my mind, build a case for a specific answer, and then seek to convince others of the merits of that approach, without really listening to feedback. Those old habits are actually a very arrogant approach that assumes that, once you have decided on the answer, there is nobody who can help you make it better. This is seldom the case.

Whenever I take the time to step back and put my

thoughts into a hypothesis and foster open debate by asking people to help me think it through and make it better, I find that I get value from that discussion and the answer ends up being better. More important, this process allows me to share ownership and responsibility for the work with the team.

A few years ago, when I was named president of the professional business for Kimberly-Clark, I implemented an approach that I now use every time I take on a big new challenge. I wrote a rough draft of the change agenda I believed was required, but I did not formalize it. I then used that rough draft agenda to help guide interviews with the entire leadership team.

I began each interview by sharing the early thoughts I had written down, but then I asked them to challenge that agenda, to add new priorities, eliminate some, and to help prioritize and focus each element of the agenda. After about ten interviews, the agenda was not changing much, so I synthesized the team's input into a very concise plan, but without locking it down, as I would have in the past. Instead, I asked my leadership team to work on that agenda together for another few weeks without me in the process. Finally, I scheduled a long working session for us to regroup and finalize it together.

When I finally got the chance to see the additional changes the team had contributed, I was really excited. The basic themes had not changed much. It was synthesized from interviews with them, after all. However, they had adapted the wording and the messages in a way that was much more relevant to the organization.

In addition, they had helped make the action steps more realistic and specific, so that we had a much better understanding of what was required to deliver on the plan. But most important, they had made the plan their own. By giving them the chance to mold it, prioritize it, and add detail to it, the team members now saw the plan as their plan—not my plan. By releasing the transformation agenda for the business and allowing the entire team to take ownership for it, I did more than just build a better agenda; I made it possible to build a better and more aligned team.

I continue to work on releasing my agenda today, and I ask the leaders who work with me to do the same. I focus time and attention on this skill because I want the best answer for the company and for my team—not just the answer that I like.

In my most recent position with Kimberly-Clark, I sent an e-mail to my leadership team to encourage them to practice this method along with me. It was a strong-willed team whose members had firm opinions, much like me, and I hoped that putting my feelings into words would make a difference for them.

> Subject: Release Your Agenda
>
> We have come a long way over the last year. Ideas are moving and spreading faster than ever across the company; we are more aligned than ever; and we rally around challenges in a manner that is really inspiring. That being said, I think we can still be better. We can take our team and teamwork to a higher level of performance, and now is the time to do that.
>
> My suggestion for making this happen is for all of us to *Release Our Agendas* when we enter into every conversation or meeting. This is something I have been

practicing, although it does not come naturally to me, but it is a very simple concept that can be very powerful.

The idea is this: If you enter into a conversation or problem-solving discussion with an agenda for an outcome you want, then you are not really listening or problem-solving with the other participants. Instead, you are trying to convince them that you are right, that your ideas are right and somehow better than the ideas they might have.

When we enter into a conversation or meeting this way, we do not build trust; we diminish it. The people we are working with will not feel heard, they will not feel like they are openly problem-solving with us, and they may feel manipulated or railroaded.

But if we enter into every conversation with a conscious effort to release our agendas and simply find the best answer for the team and the company, allowing ourselves to learn from the people we are working with, it changes the dynamic of the meeting. Suddenly, it becomes easier to listen to and evaluate options. It becomes easier to adopt and adapt ideas and easier to understand the alternative perspectives on a problem.

The key change is this: If we can manage to release our agendas and openly problem-solve with the person or team we are working with, we will hear their best ideas and have the opportunity to include that in our thinking. We can still challenge the thinking, and we should. We can still argue for an alternative approach, and we should.

In this process, we open ourselves to a range of potential outcomes, and even if the final outcome is only a marginal change from the outcome we expected, the team we are working with will feel completely different about our level of engagement with them.

It is a hard concept to put into words, but I ask that all of us work on this together. Be aware when you are entering into a problem-solving discussion with a specific agenda, a predetermined outcome you want, and be willing to release that agenda. Open yourself to a range of outcomes that includes your existing thinking, and ask the team or individual to help you think through those possibilities and options. I guarantee that the people you work with will notice the change immediately.
Chris

I shared these ideas with the team because I felt that we were failing to leverage the great talent that surrounded us. Our team was made up of headstrong leaders who were confident in themselves and their agendas, which is mostly a good thing; but they were not fully listening to the talented people who worked with and for us. As a result, we were missing out on some of those people's ideas and insights, and I wanted to challenge the team to change that reality.

The key learning for me is as follows: As leaders, we are surrounded by talented people who are eager to contribute and make a difference, and we owe it to them and to ourselves to get the most out of this talent and capability. In my experience, there are at least a few great people on every team, and our job as leaders is to engage and empower them to help shape and drive the agenda.

If we have already defined the agenda and we have no intention of listening to the input of the people we work with, then we are missing out on a fantastic opportunity to get the most out of the talent available to us. And we are effectively asking them to "shut up and do what you are told." That is not the type of leader I aspire to be.

But when we release our agendas and engage in true problem-solving with our teams, we empower them. We create space for them to bring their insight, creativity, initiative, and passion to their work and to make a real difference. This may feel like slowing down versus the alternative of just accepting your answer as it stands and telling the team what to do, but that can be managed. It is easy to define a time frame and ask the team to dig in to help shape the agenda within that framework.

The team will understand the need to move fast, and team members will work hard to add value to the plan or approach without slowing down the decision-making process. More important, a leader who practices this approach will earn the trust and alignment of the team in the process, and that is crucial, because they will most likely be the people who implement the plan.

After many years of working on this, I find the best approach is to start with a hypothesis, share it openly with the team, and then simply ask a few questions. Ask if there is a big idea that is missing from the plan. Ask the team if the plan is pragmatic enough. Ask if the plan has too many priorities and whether it needs to be more focused. Ask what the barriers will be to implementing the ideas in the plan.

Good questions, asked in a genuine and transparent way, can drive a great dialogue and elicit ideas that can improve the answers. Finally, never forget to ask what you can do to help the team successfully implement the plan. Ask what barriers you can help clear for the team.

Ask when you should check back in with them to assess progress.

Ambitious and aggressive leaders approach every problem with a clear bias for action, which is a good thing. Leaders like this push the team forward and force decision-making so that teams can take action. I am blessed with this trait, and it has served me well throughout my career, but with it comes a potential blind spot that must be managed. People with this bias often lock down the agenda early and focus on convincing the people around them. Their natural tendency will be to shut down problem-solving and input in the process. For those of you who relate to this style, my suggestion is to practice releasing your agenda in key meetings and problem-solving sessions. If you can adjust your style and open up your agenda for real debate and input, you will get more out of the talented people that surround you. And you will earn their trust and respect. It will be worth the effort.

CHAPTER 4

Drop the Baggage

If you are like most people, you are carrying around a lot of what is popularly known as extra baggage—not physical bags, but emotional baggage, which tends to travel with us throughout our lives and careers. This baggage has many sources and many forms. It could be negative feelings toward a rival or a boss; it could derive from anger or disappointment with company leadership; it might be driven by your perspective of company strategy; or it might simply be the accumulated emotion you have amassed based on how you have been treated by the company or organization where you work. Whatever the source, the baggage you carry based upon past experiences is very real, and it can affect your current and future leadership actions in a meaningful way.

Coming to terms with this baggage, so that you can refocus on the future and drive positive change, can be challenging. We may have very valid reasons for feeling anger or frustration with a person or an organization, but those feelings are about the past. If we are investing our time feeling anger and frustration about the past, which we cannot change, then we are not investing that time and energy thinking about the future, which we have the opportunity to change.

I have made the mistake of allowing feelings of anger and frustration about past events affect my ability to add value and create a better future for myself and my company. One situation that stands out for me occurred when I joined McKinsey & Company as an associate principal in 2001. I made this move after I had served as president and CEO of a small turnaround company based in Tulsa. My initial goal in joining McKinsey was to rebuild my problem-solving rigor—and to get myself back onto the radar screen of executive search firms once I made partner. However, I completely underestimated what it would take to successfully make the transition back to consulting after running a small company and being the "top dog."

As I joined the firm, I had no network of partners to bring me into client situations, and work was drying up fast following the end of the so-called Internet bubble that had led many consulting firms to expand aggressively during the late 1990s. As a result, I had limited initial success penetrating the consumer practice network. Although I had worked in consumer-facing industries for most of my career, I was going through a humbling experience of proving myself as an associate, an engagement manager, and then finally as an associate principal on a project for a large chemical company. I was feeling underappreciated and unwanted, and I was carrying those feelings around like excess baggage.

Somewhere during the course of this initiation with the firm, I attended a consumer leadership meeting that McKinsey hosted in Chicago. The meeting was a gathering of most of the principals and associate principals who served consumer-facing clients at the firm, and I saw it as a great chance to build my network. But I walked into that meeting with way too much baggage, and as a result, the wrong attitude.

As I engaged in the meeting and watched other partners share the work they were leading with their clients, I got it in my head that I needed to prove my potential value and the depth of my industry knowledge, and in the process, I made an ass of myself. I let those feelings of being underappreciated drive my behavior in that meeting, which did absolutely nothing for me.

For example:

- I openly criticized some of the client work that was presented by other consultants—and I did it in a condescending way.
- I dropped in unnecessary details just to show that I had "been there and done that" as a leader at Guinness and in my last role, leading an outsource manufacturer for major beverage companies.
- I interrogated presenters in a manner that was not helpful for the discussion and was simply designed to showcase the depth of my knowledge, but which failed to add much value for the rest of the audience.

In short, instead of building my network, I alienated a number of the senior partners at the meeting with my behavior. It was an inauspicious beginning, and it was driven by the emotion I was feeling about having to take a step back after being president of a small company, along with the baggage I was building up based upon the fact that I thought my skills were underappreciated at a firm like McKinsey. It is a great example of how our feelings about the past can influence the decisions and actions that will affect our future. Nobody in that room in Chicago had any knowledge or involvement in my personal situation, and yet I let my feelings about how I had been received at the firm drive my actions in a way that actually undermined my potential to connect with them and create opportunities to serve their clients.

Over time, I found my niche at the firm at the intersection of the operations and consumer practices. I was elected a partner in 2003 and thoroughly enjoyed that role until I finally left the firm in 2008. But I clearly had a rough start, and I made my entry into the firm more difficult than it needed to be because I let emotional baggage affect my behavior and weigh me down. If I had been truly centered at that moment in time, I would have been able to focus on the future opportunity to build my network at the firm—and I would have left any baggage about the past at the door. This might have allowed for a very different approach:

- I could have complimented the positive aspects of the work I was exposed to in the main meeting and offered a few simple ideas to add even more value.
- I could have invested more time in discussions outside the room with partners who were working on clients in whom I was interested.
- I could have grabbed some private time with the senior partners at the meeting to get their advice and coaching on how to build my network at the firm and add value to the practice.

This approach would have changed the dynamic dramatically, and it probably would have helped accelerate my path to partner at the firm. But I was incapable of executing this because I let my feelings about the past affect my actions. I was carrying around emotional baggage about how I was received at the firm and whether my potential value was being leveraged to the fullest. Ultimately, I let that baggage play a role in determining my future.

I have seen this happen many times during the course of my career. I constantly see young leaders behave in almost inexplicable ways. When I finally sit down and talk with them about it, I uncover all kinds of baggage and past emotions that are affecting their ability to be effective leaders. I remember hiring one leader who was smart, aggressive, and rigorous. He could get any project done efficiently, but he carried around a huge amount of baggage about the past that managed to sabotage him, no matter how competent he was at leading projects.

For his entire life, both personally and in his work life, he had felt unappreciated and undervalued, and he was constantly reliving these feelings. This led to some incredibly self-destructive behavior at key times. He was a master of the loud and unnecessary comment designed to draw attention, and he was constantly complaining about what the company had screwed up or failed to do for him.

It was an interesting dichotomy: here was a very competent professional whom I could entrust with any project, and yet he was constantly irritating people with behavior that was out of context. But he had such strong feelings about the past and how he had been treated that he simply could not let those feelings go and focus intensely on the future he wanted to create for himself at the company. I tried to help him with these issues, pointing out how a little self-control could go a long way toward unlocking his potential and allowing him to move faster in his career, but in crucial moments, he continued to make the same mistakes, regardless of the coaching I provided.

I have watched numerous people wrestle with this challenge, and I have come to realize just how hard letting go of the past can be. We all have accumulated experiences and strong feelings and emotions about the past, whatever that past may have been, and those emotions affect our behavior in the present. The problem is that the behavior it drives is often not very helpful in unlocking ideas and opportunities that might create a better future.

Changing this reality takes practice and self-discipline, because the experiences you have lived through are real, and the emotions you are likely to feel are real as well. Over the years, I have leveraged the following tactics as a way to help me drop the baggage and focus on the future in my interactions with my colleagues and teams. The goal with these techniques is to open up a dialogue, so that I can explore new possibilities in a discussion, rather than retrace old territory and rekindle the past feelings and memories that add no value to our problem-solving about future potential actions.

- When I meet with a person with whom I have a negative history, I try to start by asking them what is the opportunity or possibility they think we should work on together. I try to avoid simply jumping into the work because that might lead us back to the same disagreements we have had in the past. Instead, I ask them to step back and make sure we are working on the biggest opportunities that have the potential to change the company. I

find that this creates an opportunity to start from scratch with them and make sure we are engaging in innovative ideas that might excite us both and make us work together better.
- When I meet with a project team and I am skeptical of whether the project will work or deliver value, I always try to start by asking the team, "What is the big idea that I am missing?" or "How could we leverage this project to transform the company?" This tends to get the team members to think big about what they are working on, and it creates an opportunity for me to get excited about something that I otherwise would have written off as a waste of time, based on my past experience.
- Whenever I am discussing a strategy or action that is contentious and has been considered multiple times but not implemented, I always try to initiate the discussion by asking, "What has changed in our environment or business that might make this idea possible now?" The goal is to take the focus off of the past argument or disagreement that might have divided the group and instead open the conversation up to see if something has fundamentally changed in our environment that might lead us to a new conclusion.
- Finally, when I find myself locked in a disagreement with a person or a team over a decision, rather than simply support my position by talking louder or faster, I try to get the team to look a little farther into the future and answer the question, "What do you think we need to look like in five years, and what will it take to win versus our competitors at

that point in time?" I then ask the team to work backward to the immediate decisions by asking, "What do we have to do now in order to get to that future state?" I have learned that focusing on a future state and working backward takes away some of the pressure or feelings of failure people might experience if we begin to question strategies or actions they have personally championed in the past, because it is easier to accept that your past decisions or strategies may no longer be relevant in five years.

I am sure that there are many other techniques that would be effective as well. The goal is to take the focus off of our past emotions, feelings, and opinions, and instead look forward into the future and ask ourselves, "Where are we going? What are the biggest and best ideas to get us there, and what can we start doing now to get the organization moving in the right direction?" The more the conversation centers on future possibilities rather than past decisions and allegiances, the more the team can openly problem-solve the options, ideas, and potential actions.

The key in all of this is to shine a light on yourself and make sure that you are consistently pointing the discussion or the team into the future. If you are reliving past experiences and problem-solving within the framework of your past beliefs and emotions, then it will be impossible to open up new ideas and possibilities. Instead, you will simply fight old battles that have little to do with the future you are trying to create. Make sure you avoid these missteps:

- Reliving old disagreements with colleagues that have no relevance to the future

- Defending past strategies that you feel vested in
- Taking sides among functions, teams, and leaders with whom you have been aligned (or not aligned) in the past

None of these approaches creates any value. They will not help you develop any new ideas or strategies that might change the future. Rather, they simply retrace past arguments, debates, and rivalries and paralyze teams and organizations.

Getting into the right future-focused mindset—and staying there—takes work. This is because you will feel anger, you will feel frustration, you will have strong opinions that are hard to let go of, and you will have myriad other emotions and feelings that will make it hard to let go of the past. Those feelings will not add much value to your work or create new possibilities for you, but they may be powerful—and they can be hard to overcome.

If you really want to make a positive change, you have to let your desire to win in the future prevail over any historic feelings you may have about the people or company involved. It may not be easy, but if you can find a way to check the baggage at the door when you walk into your next team meeting or problem-solving session, it will make a huge difference in your ability to add value to the discussion. And if you can get the people around you to do the same, magic will happen.

So, the next time you are feeling anger or frustration about a situation or the lack of progress your team is making, try to get the team to stop, elevate above the waves of emotion and past experiences, and focus on the future. Get them to think big about what they could do if they were completely unconstrained, and see if that unlocks some new thinking and ideas.

And if you have a team member who is carrying around old baggage that is limiting his or her contributions or career progression as a result, be courageous enough to bring it up with that person and explore the reasons for the limiting behavior. I do this by asking about the emotions being experienced right after an outburst or incongruent action occurs, and I try to get the team member to focus on the "source of the baggage" and how it is affecting behavior in the moment.

There is no exact formula for exploring these issues with a team member or colleague, but if you can help the individual understand how his or her behavior may be self-defeating and then dig into why he or she feels the need to respond in a self-destructive way, it will often unlock a very honest and important conversation about the baggage being carried and how it affects the individual's behavior in the present. This may lead to an emotionally charged discussion because there may be strong feelings underpinning the behaviors in question, but confronting these issues in a direct but empathetic way may lead to real breakthroughs for your team if you are courageous enough to take them on.

CHAPTER 5

Listen for the Gold

If you are anything like me, you probably make up your mind about people pretty fast. It is often not intentional and is genuinely not meant to be mean-spirited, but it happens, usually within about five to ten minutes of meeting someone. I assume that this is human nature. We all look for traits in others that we like or dislike, and once we think we have confirmed those traits in somebody, we begin to form our assessment.

When I meet someone who is high-energy, articulate, quick, aggressive, accountable, and has some degree of self-awareness (something that came slowly to me), I immediately lean in and listen. If the individual can then demonstrate those traits consistently over time, I am hooked, and I am likely to give him or her more of my time and focus.

Conversely, when I meet someone who lacks these traits, someone who lacks energy, or is subject to being easily distracted, I tune out. Likewise for people who naturally tend to focus on the negatives and fail to recognize the positives, or seems to be slow to process information, or worse, someone who appears to blame others for the problems encountered. I am prone to quickly making up my mind that a person has nothing to offer me—no big or exciting idea—and I stop listening. I would not mention that I have stopped listening; I would just push to end the discussion quickly, and I would be reluctant to give the individual more of my time in the future.

I accept this as a natural part of who I am, and I try to work on countering it. I force myself to stay engaged even when I have already made a negative read on someone, but it remains a struggle for me. This has certainly gotten me into trouble at times in my career, because I have missed out on some great feedback and ideas from people whose opinion I had already discounted. I often fail to listen for the gold that people can offer me, the experience they can share, and the ideas they may have because I have already made up my mind about them, and this limits my ability to listen intently. I have made this mistake many times throughout my career—too many to count, unfortunately—but the best example I can remember occurred during my tenure at Guinness.

After a year working as the vice president of strategy for the Americas region, I took a role as the general manager for the Latin America division of Guinness. It was a small business that was distributed across many countries and with many go-to-market models. We were brewing our beer locally in markets like Panama, Belize, and El Salvador, and negotiating a similar arrangement in Chile.

We were importing premium packaged products into markets like Argentina and Brazil, and we were looking at opening up pubs and a draft business in cities like Buenos Aires and Sao Paolo. It was a very small business, but it was incredibly diverse, and we had great latitude to test alternative models in order to determine the best strategy to grow the business in the long term.

I moved to South Florida to start my new job, a location from which a number of multinational companies ran their Latin American businesses at that time. Around the time of my move, a new leader for Guinness's overall Caribbean/Latin America business was appointed, and this leader moved down to Boca Raton, Florida, where our office was located.

We began to frame the strategy for the region together, but I quickly began to develop opinions of him that got in the way of my ability to listen and learn from him. In my thirty-one-year-old brain, I was convinced that this first real operating role was my chance to really define myself as an aggressive leader who was capable of transforming businesses, and I wanted to "go big or go home" in terms of our growth strategy.

My new boss was a more seasoned and pragmatic leader who had been with Guinness for some time. He knew that our product and our brand development model were unique and that it typically took many years to build a strong foundation. As a result, he believed that the best approach was to experiment with various entry models, take our time assessing the performance and potential of each model, and then to leverage those learnings to frame the investment case in a couple of years. This was not an unreasonable strategy, but to me it felt timid and slow. I wanted to invest ahead of the curve and refine the strategy as we went along.

As I spent more time working with my new boss, I developed an increasingly negative opinion of him, and I became less open to his ideas and insights. I felt that he was being measured and conservative for the wrong reasons, in particular to protect his lush lifestyle. He clearly loved the benefits of living in South Florida, playing golf and traveling to the great locations in our region.

The more I observed him, the more I made up my mind that he was not the kind of leader I wanted to partner with. Despite the fact that he had substantial experience in the business, I simply saw a leader who was overly cautious and conservative. Even worse, I felt that he was highly political in terms of how he positioned himself at the company, and I questioned whether he would support me if and when we faced challenges.

But there was a fundamental problem with my thinking. Although some of my observations about this person may have been correct, I became so dismissive of him as a leader that I missed the opportunity to leverage his experience and his ideas, which might have helped my team improve the business.

I failed to listen for the gold, in terms of what he had to offer, and that resulted in a number of avoidable mistakes. I was a very young leader taking on my first real operating role. I knew very little about building brands, leading a sales team, or managing partner relationships. He had substantial experience doing all of those things. He knew the tough questions to ask about brand development; he knew how to interpret research results and account penetration data; and he knew how to manage within the organizational hierarchy of the company.

On paper, you might have thought we would be a perfect combination—the smart, aggressive young leader paired with the experienced brand builder who had helped develop the brand from its early days in North America. But we never turned out to be that winning team.

I remember a number of trips we made to the markets together. He would ask very good questions—about repeat purchase by account and how we were investing our marketing resources to build a loyal core—questions that I could have answered with a little work and which would have uncovered important insights into the health of the business. My reaction was to become defensive.

Instead of seeing this as an opportunity to learn and improve our approach, I defended the work that had been done and became even more intransigent in my opinion of him. I look back now and feel embarrassed that I had become so fixed in my opinion of my boss that I could not listen to the perfectly reasonable issues he was raising and insights he offered. Some of the reason for that may have been his style, but I have to be accountable for the missed opportunity, because I made up my mind about him early on in our relationship and after that point, I failed to listen for the gold. I failed to leverage the experience he could have offered me.

In the end, many of the concerns he raised and issues he identified with our growth strategy turned out to be accurate, and the business struggled as a result. My experience there was not a failure, but the explosive growth I was counting on to rocket my career at Guinness never materialized. As I look back now, the most interesting irony is that I wanted to go big and go fast in order to hit a home run, and I stopped listening to my boss because I thought he would slow us down with his conservative and politically-savvy approach.

In the process, I failed to leverage his experience and ideas that could have helped me address the very issues that ended up slowing us down. I let my feelings about him

For the most part, they had already made up their minds about the people they were meeting and the ideas that were being shared. In each case, they found a reason why those ideas and insights should not be considered relevant.

In frustration, I finally asked the team if there was anyone with a perspective on the business that was different from their own from whom they thought they could learn. The only response I can remember was a long, awkward silence.

The point I am trying to make is simply this: Once you make up your mind about a person or a group based upon traits or indicators that seem different than those you are familiar or comfortable with, you are likely to stop listening for the gold. No matter what the reasoning is for excluding these ideas and insights—they are too quirky, too strange, too creative, too aggressive, too conservative, or too unrealistic—if you consistently decide to dismiss the ideas of people who are different from you and your team, you will miss out on some big ideas and opportunities in the process.

As a senior executive, I have to work hard at trying to listen for the gold in every interaction. I try to introduce my team to new experiences with people who are very different from us, who might stimulate new ideas and insights. This takes focus and effort, as my natural bias to judge the people I am meeting with can take over quickly. But I push myself to get at least one big idea from every meeting and every interaction.

I typically try to do this by listening for ten to fifteen minutes and then asking the team, "Help me understand the big idea—how will this idea or project change the company in a meaningful way and make us more successful?" Or I might ask the team, "Help me understand what I might be missing," and then I will very transparently describe my first reaction, even if it is negative, and ask them to explain to me what I am not seeing. I try to do this in a non-threatening way, so that the team feels empowered to challenge my thinking and to sell me on their ideas.

Although there are times that I still fail to see the "big idea," I find that this approach allows me to open up the dialogue with the team, and it takes the pressure off the presentation, instead engendering a more casual discussion about how any idea could be a big idea. Even if the answer is that there is no "big idea," that itself is a discovery the team needs to make.

I work just as hard at challenging my team to be open to new ideas from external sources. At every leadership team meeting, I try to schedule time for field trips to leading companies in a range of industries that might be able to share ideas and strategies that are different from our own. My challenge to the team is the same—try to listen for the gold—try to get "one big idea" from each meeting that you can use as you run your business. The goal is not to dictate what they take away from these external meetings, but rather to challenge them to keep learning and keep listening for the gold.

We once visited a very successful Internet retailer and a leading casino operator on the same trip. The two companies could not have been more different. The Internet retailer looked nothing like our company. The offices were a mess; the associates were dressed very differently from what we were used to; the team was small and team members mostly knew each other; and their business model was completely different from ours. And yet, it was a great lens into how quickly business is changing and how we need to change in order to attract the next generation of talent.

On the other hand, the casino operation was the polar opposite. It was a very large and structured operation with thousands of unionized service workers. But the operating leader there had some fabulous ideas and practices designed to inspire and focus the entire organization to deliver a distinctive level of service in a very competitive market. He was using simple daily messages to connect with his team members and focus their energy, and he had a number of interesting ways of celebrating the right behaviors and actions in order to reinforce the goals and values of the company.

Every day I go to work, every meeting I participate in, and every time I visit a market, I try to listen for the gold. I am by no means proficient at it, but I constantly work at it. In my experience, we are surrounded by big insights and great ideas, but we have to be open to them. We have to find ways to get new people and new ideas into our daily dialogue so that we can stay in touch with the world around us and keep our businesses relevant in a rapidly changing world. Sometimes those ideas will come from people who are radically different from us.

My worry is that most senior executives would get at best a grade of C- or a D, if we were grading on this skill. They get so comfortable with their position, so confident in their knowledge of the business, so firm in their opinions about which people add value and which don't, and so set in their ways, that they stop listening for the gold, and they fail to open themselves up to the changes that are driving the marketplace around them. This is a dangerous reality for both them and the companies they lead.

CHAPTER 6

Humility and the Art of Asking for Help

I remember feeling completely overwhelmed when I began my career at the Boston Consulting group. I knew almost nothing about business, management consulting, or the business analyst job I had been hired to do. After moving to Chicago and settling into my new apartment, I literally could not sleep for an entire week. I was so nervous and so excited to be joining a highly regarded and demanding company like BCG that I could not stop my mind from running all night long.

That first day of work, I got to the building early, and once the receptionist let me into the BCG offices, I wandered the halls looking for my nameplate on a cube or office. It turned out that the second-year analysts had decided to play a joke on me the night before, and they had moved my nameplate to the office of the lead partner for the Midwest region at the time.

It was surprising to me that the company would give such a large office to a new analyst, but I dropped my bag and settled into the comfortable chair, only to stand back up a few minutes later when the managing partner walked in and made me aware of the trick the team had played on me. He was good-natured about it, though, and at least I got the chance to meet him on my first day.

Later that week, I was assigned to my first project team. I do not remember the client or the project, but I spent thirty minutes with the engagement manager while he outlined the research and analysis he wanted me to do, and I launched into it. My first couple of weeks on the project team were a matter of trial and error. I would complete some work and try to capture it on a couple of slides, and then I would circle back with the engagement manager to get feedback. Most of my initial work was of little value. It was quickly thrown out, and I was sent back to my desk to redo it. At the end of three weeks of work, I think only two of my analyses made it to the final client presentation, but it was exciting to be on a team and working on what seemed like important issues.

I eventually started to learn the role and the expectations of a consultant, and it was rewarding to see that more of my work output started finding its way into key client discussions. But as I look back on those first few months, I wonder why I did not invest more time asking for help and guidance from the amazing people who were in that office. The company was full of smart people, all of whom had gone through a similar experience just a few years before. Every one of them would have been willing to provide ideas and advice if I had bothered to ask. There are so many simple things I could have done:

- Every time I got a new assignment, I could have asked three or four people what they would do if they were in my shoes.

- Every time I began to think about how to capture the output of my analysis, I could have asked a few people whether they had seen similar work before and how they would suggest I synthesize the work.
- Every time I was problem-solving the outcome of interviews and market research, I could have captured my initial ideas on a whiteboard and asked others to give me feedback.

A few people might have responded that they were too busy to help, but I would bet that at least 70 percent would have happily given me ten to fifteen minutes of their time. And asking those questions would have supplied me with great ideas and guidance that would have substantially improved my work and output. However, I was reluctant to ask for help. Even when I was completely stuck, I could not get myself to wander the office in search of ideas and advice.

At first, I think I was worried that people would look down on me or question my skills if I asked for help all of the time. Then, as I began to develop some proficiency, I think I assumed that I did not need (or should not need) the help any more. Whatever the case, I failed to take full advantage of the incredible people and the amazing ideas that surrounded me at work every day. These were intellectually curious people who would have been more than willing to problem-solve and share their experience with me. I was either too insecure or too arrogant to leverage their knowledge.

Over the years, I have learned this lesson and forgotten it many times. A dozen years after leaving BCG, I joined McKinsey & Company as an associate principal. There is no doubt that my analytical skills and presentation skills were a little rusty when I jumped back into consulting after more than a decade of working at various operating companies. But as I went through the humbling initiation process of serving briefly as an associate, then an engagement manager, and finally as an associate principal, I struggled with capturing my ideas and my team's analyses in a compelling manner. I was simply out of practice, and I was unfamiliar with the standard practices at McKinsey that anyone who had started as an associate with the firm would have learned years before.

But once again, I found myself reluctant to ask for help. I think this time it was ego. I was used to being the boss at a small company, and I was embarrassed to ask consultants ten years my junior for advice. But this proved to be another lost opportunity. I had quickly developed a relationship with a number of talented people in the office, and they would have been more than willing to help me with structure and format and other ideas and insights, if I had asked them. They valued the real operating experience and leadership development insights that I could share with them, and I am sure they would have "leaned in" to help me, if I had been humble enough to share my situation openly with them.

This is the big insight I would like to share with you: In every situation or company where you may work, you are likely to be surrounded by bright people who are willing to provide guidance, problem-solve your work, or simply share advice, but you have to be willing to ask in order to get full value from all of that insight and experience.

You may feel like you should already know the answer, or that people will look down on you if you ask them to share their ideas, but I have found just the opposite to be true. Whenever I ask people to show me how they do things or to share their ideas, they typically light up with excitement. They want to feel valued, and most of the time they love the fact that you want to listen and learn from them. I know that when someone asks me for help with a tough challenge or issue, I am always excited to dig into the issue with them and problem-solve a few ideas that might drive change. I might have to ask them to come back a little later when I have free time, but it is never an imposition.

Despite this fact, I see leaders ignoring and wasting the talent and experience around them all of the time. Perhaps the most egregious example I can remember happened just recently when I worked with a newly hired senior leader who joined a mid-sized company from a different industry. He was a really smart executive with some great new ideas and an amazing background of experience to draw upon. But he was hired into a senior operating role in a business that was new to him.

You would think that a confident leader would immediately start by trying to learn as much as he could about the industry from the other veterans on the leadership team. There were a number of leaders with thirty years or more of experience that he could have tapped and from whom he could have learned:

- He could have traveled with them to local operations to learn the market through their eyes.
- He could have attended their monthly business review meetings to understand their business challenges and their plans to address the issues and opportunities.

- He could have summarized the problems that were occurring in his own business and reviewed those with other leaders to gain from their experience and evaluate potential solutions.
- He could have asked them to attend a couple of his operating meetings and provide ideas and feedback.

But he did none of these things. Instead, he holed up in his office, traveled alone, and kept all of his ideas and work to himself. He probably felt like it would be a sign of weakness to ask for help, so he chose to go it alone—despite constant coaching to open himself up and benefit from the experience of the rest of the leadership team.

Not surprisingly, this did not end well. The executive lasted just nine months in his new role before the CEO decided he had seen enough and asked him to leave. His team barely reacted when it found out that he would be released. He had not asked team members for their ideas either, so they did not feel connected with him in any way.

I am confident that this leader had the potential to succeed in the role he was hired into, but he was in a new industry, facing new issues and challenges, and he needed to open himself up to new ideas, experiences, and learning. It is a very simple but very powerful lesson that I have learned over time, that no matter how junior or how senior you are, you have the right and the opportunity to ask questions and pursue new ideas and insights. It is not a sign of weakness; it is simply evidence of your intellectual curiosity and fundamental desire to learn from your colleagues and your team.

I try to leverage this opportunity every time I take on a new challenge. Over the last five years, I have been lucky enough to be entrusted with three senior operating roles. The first was president of Kimberly-Clark Professional; the second was president of Kimberly-Clark International; and recently I became COO of Sally Beauty Holdings, Inc. In the first two cases, I started by investing substantial time and energy in asking questions and asking for help, and I fully intend to apply the same approach at Sally Beauty. I try to invest that time in the following manner:

- To begin with, I start by discussing the new opportunity with key stakeholders, such as the CEO, the outgoing leader, and key board members to get initial ideas and insights. I typically capture a rough draft of the ideas we discuss in those meetings in handwritten notes. I intentionally do not produce any formal documents because I want to avoid sending the message that my mind is made up on any issue or idea.
- Then, I typically interview the top fifteen or twenty leaders on my direct team. In each interview, I share my handwritten notes and ask them to provide additional ideas, as well as to refine the ideas that have already been shared. The interviews of the senior team typically take two or three weeks, and they allow me to listen intently to each leader and their ideas. These interviews also provide terrific initial insight into the strength and weaknesses of the team.
- Next, I capture the ideas of the team on a couple of pages titled "Our Change Agenda." It would normally be divided into a case for change, with a rough vision and set of aspirational goals; the key agenda priorities (action steps) the team has

identified; and the leadership behaviors the team believes will be required from the organization in order to succeed. I try to limit this document to a page or two, as it needs to be simple and pragmatic if we are going to use it to engage the organization.

- Once a draft change agenda is captured, I typically ask my team to take it with them for two or three weeks and to ask their direct reports to provide feedback. I would also ask them to look at what competitors and other industries are doing that might provide us with ideas and insights. I want them to get comfortable presenting the agenda and opening themselves up to the ideas and insights of their teams
- After they have completed this task, I assemble the entire team face-to-face for at least one full day, two days if necessary, but no more, to integrate our thoughts. I ask the team to share what new ideas have surfaced, what issues or barriers have been identified, what might I have overlooked because I am new to the business and lack their experience, and then we work on rewriting the agenda together. The objective is to capture the biggest ideas and debate the priorities in real time. But I insist that we walk out of that meeting with a change agenda with which we are all aligned and which we all support.
- Once the agenda is complete, we use it to set financial targets for the organization and integrate that into our bonus plans. We build a dashboard to track the key initiatives and discuss our results and our progress on those initiatives

at every leadership meeting. We use that agenda to update the board or the corporate team on how we are doing, what is working, and what remains challenging.
- Finally, every six months, I ask the team to invest another day to update the agenda. We ask ourselves whether the issues and priorities are still relevant and whether we have learned anything new from the marketplace or competition that would make us adapt the agenda to the new circumstances. We also try to visit leading organizations from outside our industry to see if we can learn from them and include some of their best practices in our agenda.

This process has served me well. It allows me to ask lots of questions and listen intently to the ideas and concerns of the organization. It may seem like you are slowing down just as you are jumping into a new role, but I try to start the initial interviews two weeks before I begin my new role, and I find the team can typically align on a change agenda within six to eight weeks of my first day on the job. More important, it sends some important messages to your team:

- It shows that you are willing to listen and learn from the experience of others.
- It shows humility and indicates to the organization that you want to learn.
- It demonstrates that you value their ideas and insights.
- It highlights the importance of alignment and shared accountability.

This may feel like a time sink, but I guarantee you it will be worth the effort. When you drive a race car on a track, there is a simple axiom that a professional driver once explained to me: slow entry—fast exit. That describes how you want to set up a car to maneuver the corners. You brake before the corner and accelerate through and out of it. The same is true when you start a new job—hit the brakes for just a few days, take the time to ask for ideas and help, leverage the amazing capability and experience that surrounds you, and then hit the accelerator.

You may think you are smart enough to get started on your own, or you may worry that it will look bad if you ask others for help, but you need to put these feelings of hubris or insecurity behind you and focus on capturing the great ideas and insights of the talent around you. I promise you will discover that a little humility and curiosity can take you a long way.

CHAPTER 7

The Cruel Joke

Your career is going to play a cruel joke on you. You may not realize it at the time, but as you become more senior in your career journey, you will look back and see it.

The setup for this joke is simple: During the first ten or so years of your career, you will get very good at shining a light on yourself in order to advance, and then, as you begin to lead larger teams, you will need to pivot fast and learn how to shine the light on your team, rather than yourself. No one alerts you to the need for the shift, but if you fail to make this pivot at the right time, you will find that your teams do not like you very much.

Some people never make this pivot. I smile when I see these people, senior leaders who are still talking about themselves, how great they are, and how great their ideas are, despite the fact that they are now accomplished executives who have large teams that do the majority of the real work.

These leaders should be secure and confident enough in their own accomplishments that shifting the spotlight should come naturally. When they fail to do this, they struggle to build genuinely engaged and motivated teams, because the people who work for them will be suspicious of their willingness to support and empower the people they lead.

I experienced the initial stages of this transition or pivot about ten years into my career. Early in my career, I was very accomplished at shining a light on myself. This will come as no surprise to people who worked with me. Although I made plenty of mistakes along the way, I was generally very good at presentations. I was very confident and comfortable in front of senior audiences, and I had no issues with speaking up in key meetings.

Perhaps most important, I was very good at interviewing, which meant I presented myself very well with executive recruiters and potential new employers. That skill allowed me to progress rapidly in my career. But as I worked my way into more senior jobs and my teams got larger, I had to learn to adjust my style in order to be successful.

In my early thirties, when I led the Latin America division for Guinness, and later, when I moved on to run Whitlock Packaging, I began leading teams of people at the director and manager level, and I struggled with letting go of the limelight.

When the important presentations needed to be written and presented, or we met with outside executives at customer companies and potential investors, I wanted to lead those meetings. I rationalized this in my head as simply wanting us to do the best as a team in those important situations. But the truth is that I did not fully trust others to lead those presentations as well as I thought I could lead them.

I had substantial experience in consulting and senior

strategy roles, and I was quick on my feet in front of a crowd, so I assumed that we would be more likely to succeed if I led the tough presentations and meetings.

Although I probably could present certain materials better, I think I missed out on something with this approach. First, I failed to fully engage my team. The team never had full ownership for the strategy and the plan because I was the one who wrote it and presented it. I think my team members knew that I did not fully trust them to handle that.

Second, I missed out on the opportunity to put myself on the same side of the table as the people we were presenting to. Since I was in the front of the room selling the plan or strategy, I could not be an objective participant who was problem-solving the opportunity along with the other recipients. As I reflect back on my mindset during that time, I realize that I was always in "sell mode." I would sell my team on a strategy or approach; then I would sell it to my boss and senior leaders; and then I would sell that to external stakeholders, such as customers and investors. I authored the story and then sold it to everyone I could, and I wanted to be center stage because I knew the story better than anyone else and could present it better than anyone else.

As I look back today, I can see that I had not made the pivot to being a senior leader. I was still shining the light on myself and focusing on standing out at the right time, rather than building a genuinely strong team. What I have discovered over time is that this journey of letting go of center stage continues to evolve throughout your career path.

It begins with leading small teams, and with success, it

expands to leading very senior business leaders who craft their own strategies and plans and review those with you. As that process evolves, a leader has to evolve with it. As you get more senior, you have to give the leaders working for you more and more space in order to let them feel real ownership and accountability for a strategy or plan. If you fail to do that, it will be difficult to succeed as the scope of your responsibilities expands.

I think the experience that finally allowed me to fully let go of the microphone came when I ran the Kimberly-Clark professional division. I had spent the last two years as chief strategy officer, and I was lucky enough to be offered the opportunity to lead the $3.5 billion business-to-business segment of KC. It was an amazing business and an incredible opportunity to step up and prove myself as a line leader in a large business segment. But as I joined, the business was going through some difficult times. Volume in our largest unit was soft, and our plants were not fully utilized as a result.

Additionally, our pricing was out of line with the market on a number of product lines. Our European business was struggling in a challenging market, and our customers and channel partners were seeing us increasingly as a commodity player. As a result, our margins were declining and revenue was stagnant. Operating results were in steady decline for the first six months of my tenure.

My first reaction in the face of these headwinds was to jump in and take the reins. I launched cost programs, pricing programs, alternative fiber programs, channel management programs, innovation programs, national accounts programs, and any other program that seemed like it might move the needle on results. In addition, I handled the majority of senior leader presentations and business reviews, so that I could explain the challenges we faced and how we planned on addressing them. It was a tough time in my career, as I felt like we were pulling every lever and the business was not responding.

We finally turned the business about six months later, and results improved dramatically, but when I got my first round of feedback from the leaders who worked for me, I was surprised that it was so mixed. I got good feedback in terms of my ability to create a sense of urgency and focus the organization, but a number of senior leaders felt like I was micromanaging the organization and failing to give them sufficient space to craft their own plans and execute them.

At first I was angered by the feedback; I felt that I had done what was necessary to get the business back on track during a challenging period. But as I spoke with people across the organization, I realized that I had made the turnaround too much about me and not about the team. I had shined too much of the light on myself, and I had failed to empower and energize the people who needed to step up and take the business to the next level.

With this in mind, and with the business stabilized, we began to craft the longer-term strategy for the business with the team. But I worked hard at taking a step back and letting the team play a bigger role in defining that. I focused on the case for change— that we needed to change the business model or face continued commoditization and price erosion—and I let the working teams shape the elements of the new approach.

Instead of defining the specific agenda, I did my best to stay out of the details and simply be a sponsor for the good ideas that were emerging. We asked working teams to define the core platforms that would drive the business going forward. This culminated in a senior leader meeting in which we selected the platforms to prioritize, defined the action plan to implement them, and wrote the new vision for the business. I remember walking into that meeting, and I had my preferred vision and strategy in my head, but rather than present it, as I might have done in the past, I held back and went through the problem-solving process along with everyone else on the team.

In the end, we finalized the strategy and the vision, and the team members felt like they truly owned it. The final vision statement was different from the one I had in my head. It was better. It was not my strategy, it was **our** strategy, and that made all of the difference. From that point on, we began to make huge progress driving the business to the next level of performance.

Perhaps the proudest moment came six months later, as we shared the new strategy and transformation plan for the business at a senior leader meeting for all of KC. I did not present a thing (I think I got to introduce the team). The team presented the strategy, the transformation plan, the new sales and marketing approach, and the new vision for the company.

That presentation ended with my entire team coming up on stage while a video that explained the vision played in the background. It was clear to everyone at that meeting that the team owned this strategy: it was their business; team members were proud to be leading it; and they were completely accountable for delivering on the results. I did not need to say a thing. The light was shining completely on them, and that was perfect.

This is a hard pivot to make. It requires trust in your team, confidence in yourself, and a genuine willingness to problem-solve with your team, rather than presenting to your team or telling team members what to do.

I have seen many leaders struggle with this change. When they get to their first large-scale leadership role, they want to do the right thing. They want their teams to be excited and energized, but they fail to create enough space and freedom within a framework for the team to do that.

I saw a presentation recently by Gary Hamel, an influential business thinker, and he talked about how most companies only get compliance and diligence from their people because they have so much structure, so many rules, and such rigid processes that they fail to leave room for imagination, creativity, initiative, and passion. Weak leaders do the same thing. They are so worried about giving away the spotlight and something going wrong that they fail to fully trust and engage their teams.

I remember working with a very senior leader at a large client company I served while at McKinsey. He always wanted the spotlight, and he wanted everything to be perfect all the time. Every presentation had to be perfect, and he had to review it well in advance in order to get it just right. He had to lead every financial review, communicate current performance, and defend the team's plan to overcome any gaps. In addition, he had to be the one on stage for all of the really important meetings with the CEO or the board.

He worked outrageously long hours and did his best to stay on top of the details, and his team just hated working for him. He did not think that was true, but when I got to know his team members, it was clear that none of them would willingly work for this person.

Leaders like this suck the energy out of an organization. They create performance management processes that are all about keeping them informed in the event that they need to answer for the CEO or the board. However, this type of process has nothing to do with running the business better. In fact it does the opposite.

The organization gets so focused on pleasing the leader, making sure the leader looks good in the right meetings, making sure the leader is happy with presentations and plans, and making sure the leader is always up to speed on key initiatives, that the team loses focus on what really matters—building the business and winning in the marketplace relative to competitors. Even more important, the team members will often lose their energy and enthusiasm for the work over time, because pleasing the boss is not nearly as engaging as building a successful business or company.

If you want to be a great leader, if you want your team members to invest their imagination, creativity, initiative, and passion into their work, and not just their diligence and compliance, then you have to take the spotlight off yourself and put it on them. This will seem scary at first. It will feel like you are giving up control, and it will feel like you are taking a risk. However, the real risk and the real mistake is trying to personally own and control the entire leadership process. Because you cannot do it. You cannot lead a large organization and control everything: it simply is not possible. Great leaders build and inspire great teams. They pick great people; they engage them with a compelling case for change and vision for the future; and then they get out of the way and shine the spotlight on them.

Great leaders thrive on their teams' success, they feel energized and inspired seeing others succeed, and they cannot wait to spotlight that success within the organization and see those leaders move on to bigger roles. If you cannot create sufficient space to let the team define its own agenda, test its own ideas, and experience and learn from both success and failure, then you will never get the most from your team and the team members will never see you as a great leader.

Your pivot may be coming or it may have already happened, but the time will come for every leader who advances to a senior level in an organization. There will come a time in your career when you will need to stop being the one who is always on stage and in front, and instead, learn to lead from behind.

This will require you to trust your team, so pick a good one. While it will feel like a loss of control at times, if you can master it, you can unlock the real potential of your team and create a genuinely inspiring work environment for both your team and for yourself.

CHAPTER 8

Never Burn Bridges

You might think that this is such a clichéd and obvious statement that it would be unnecessary to include a chapter on this subject in a book like this. But I have seen so many leaders mess this up that I thought I would include my thoughts on the issue. I have developed some expertise on the subject, which happens when you work for eight different companies in the first twenty-eight years of your career. Over the course of that experience, I made a few silly mistakes, but I also developed a profound appreciation for this axiom.

The premise is simple: The world is much smaller than you may think. As you get more senior in your career path, it will continue to get smaller and smaller. I think this is especially true in a wired world like today's. As a result, you want to leave the best impression you possibly can, no matter what feelings you may have about a former company, a boss, or a colleague. It sounds simple, but I have seen many people let emotion get the better of them as they move on, and this can create a negative legacy that may come back to haunt them later in their careers.

As I mentioned, I have had lots of experience at this, but I clearly remember two examples from my career where

I failed to leave the best impression. The first came early in my career, as I was building the analyst program at CSC Index in 1993. I tried to recruit potential candidates from the top-tier consulting firms, one of which was my former firm, BCG. I attempted to do this the right way, by calling the current leader of the analyst program at the firm and asking him to refer people who might be interested in working at another firm prior to business school. But when that failed to yield candidates, I asked some old friends at the firm if they could recommend anyone, and they quickly identified an ideal potential candidate.

I tried my best not to be overly aggressive with my pursuit. She was at her two-year point with the firm, and she was not sure about business school, so she was considering staying an additional year at BCG, as well as other potential options. I simply wanted to be the most attractive of those other potential options. In the end, she chose to come to work with us at CSC Index, and she quickly proved to be a fantastic hire. However, a few of the leaders at BCG felt I was overly aggressive in trying to raid talent from my former firm. I found out later in my career that I had created some negative feelings about my values and behaviors that lived on long after that situation.

At the time, I felt like this was just a healthy competition for talent that we had managed to win, but as I think back on my approach today, I would agree that I was aggressive in my tactics to identify and recruit the candidate. I wanted to win, and I pushed the boundaries. This is fine when you are fighting for talent versus a firm or company with which you have no relationship, but I think I should have held myself to a higher standard when it came to a former employer.

The second time I left on the wrong terms was a much more blatant example. After I left CSC Index, I joined Guinness/United Distillers, first as vice president of strategy and later as the general manager for the Latin America region. My last three years at Guinness were spent living in South Florida and learning fast. It was my first true operating role, and I was learning how to manage a profit and loss statement, as well as build our brands in myriad local markets. It was a great experience that I thoroughly enjoyed, but after a few years, the company went through a large-scale merger, and the work environment changed dramatically. As a result, I began looking outside the company at other opportunities.

During this difficult time, I was asked to be part of an expert panel at a global beverage forum in New York. I spoke about my experience building a fledgling business for Guinness in emerging markets. In the audience that day was the founder of a large contract manufacturer for the beverage industry, who was looking for a new president and CEO for his company. As I mentioned earlier, it can be a small world.

He listened to my presentation and gave my name to the search firm Spencer Stuart, which had been engaged to fill the position. The next week, I got a call from the executive recruiter working on the project, and soon after that I was in Tulsa, Oklahoma, interviewing for the job. It was a heady experience; I was thirty-four years old, and I was being considered for the top job at a mid-sized company with more than a thousand employees.

Over the course of the next few weeks, I went through a couple of rounds of interviews, visited Tulsa to look at housing, and eventually, I was offered the job as president and CEO of Whitlock Packaging Corporation. I got carried away with the excitement, pride, and emotion of the experience.

As I was finishing up my work with Guinness and preparing to move, I decided to write a letter to the CEO of Guinness articulating what I thought needed to be done to change the company. I did not single out any individuals, and I tried my best to offer constructive ideas, but it was a stupid thing to do. I sent the e-mail off without getting any input or feedback from my teammates or colleagues, and I bypassed two levels of management in the process.

I genuinely thought I was offering positive ideas to drive change, but as soon as my colleagues saw the letter, they immediately expressed their disappointment in me. In their view, the letter was insulting, and it failed to recognize the positive progress that was being made in a number of areas. To them, it was just a parting shot that I was firing across the bow to thumb my nose at senior leadership.

In the end, I wrote a follow-up letter, apologizing for my approach and attempting to focus on the ideas I thought were meaningful. I think it helped to some extent; at least my colleagues appreciated that I was willing to do that when I did not have to. But I would still call the decision to write the initial letter a stupid mistake. If I had been genuinely committed to driving positive change for my colleagues, I would have started by talking to them first, asking them for guidance on whether to write the letter and what content might drive the best outcome. They were the ones who were going to have to manage the aftermath; I was on my way to Tulsa.

Today, having changed jobs seven times, I would

seek to leave on the best terms possible, no matter what the circumstance. I would do my best to make sure I followed up on every key project or initiative that impacted the business and to hand that over to other leaders in the best way possible. I would invest tirelessly to make sure the transition to a new leader was as smooth as possible, helping out with internal and external communications; making sure the new leader understood all of the key financial and strategic issues and opportunities; and making sure that any business issues that came up during the transition were handled in an expedient way.

Finally, I would stay above the fray at all times. I would refuse to say anything negative about why I was leaving, and I would resist the temptation to criticize other leaders on my way out.

This approach involves biting your tongue at times, but it is the right way to handle the situation because you should aspire to be a consummate professional no matter what the circumstances.

I would do all of this for two reasons. The most important is that I care about my team members, and I want them to succeed, regardless of whether I will be part of the team going forward. I want the team to know that it was the most important thing to me and that I would do anything I could to support my team members. That approach is what will make them want to work for me again in the future or send other talented people my way.

The second reason is that the professional circle of a senior executive is very small, and I want people to know that I would never drop the ball, thumb my nose, violate my commitments to a former employer, or act in any way that was not viewed as consistent with the highest professional standards.

I want to leave them believing that I managed the transition professionally, and I want them to speak with enthusiasm about my professionalism when someone inquires about me in the future.

It requires self-discipline to accomplish the well-crafted exit, because you may have strong emotions about the situation and how you were treated or supported. However, you must put that emotion aside and focus on maintaining the highest level of professional conduct, no matter what.

To give you an example of how I handled an exit from a company, here is one of the e-mails I sent out before making my exit. This e-mail was sent out to a large number of colleagues at McKinsey & Company. I had received some pretty rough feedback and coaching from the partner review committee just a few months prior to this e-mail, but I worked hard not to let that affect my attitude or my exit. The distribution list included fifty to sixty partners, friends, and trusted team members, and the content was as follows:

> Subject: A good-bye note
>
> As I get ready to leave in a few weeks, I want you all to know how fantastic it has been to work with you over the last few years. The best part of my McKinsey experience has been the opportunity to work with people like yourselves. You make a difference for the people around you every day, and you certainly made a difference for me.
>
> Before I go, I thought I would share a few thoughts and insights that have made a difference for me over the

years. These are not meant to preach, just share. They are in no particular order.

1) Be fearless. You are some of the most special people with whom I have ever worked. There is no mistake you can make that you cannot recover from. If you believe that (and it is true), you will be courageous in the face of adversity, and you will be willing to stand for the right answer over the easy answer. The moment you genuinely trust your capabilities and stop trying to prove yourself is the moment you will be free to provide really meaningful leadership and coaching to others.

2) Be transparent. The more open you are with people, the more they will connect with you. Share your joys, your pains, your challenges. Don't try to be perfect or perfectly buttoned up all the time. Everyone knows perfection is a lie. Your colleagues and teams will trust you more, and connect with you more, if you show them the real you, warts and all.

3) Never feel sorry for yourself. You are very lucky to have the skills and talents you possess. No matter what bad luck hits, no matter what some jerk might do to you, you are still lucky. If the worst happens, just figure out what you want to do next, pick yourself up, and start doing it. Don't be afraid to reach out to your friends and colleagues for help, because good people love helping people like you. They will not see it as an imposition, and they will jump on the opportunity.

The best people I have ever met all survived a major setback in their careers and came out better for it in the end. It will happen to you as well; just accept that fact. You will prove more about yourself by recovering from the big mistake or challenge than by trying to avoid it.

4) Put your faith in your team. McKinsey can become way too focused on individual performance, such as standing out in front of clients or in a problem-solving session with CST leadership. The result is that it is easy to lose focus on the power of a great team. When we provide real leadership to our teams, which means providing them with clear direction and insightful coaching and inspiration, and then getting out of their way, the team will make magic happen every time. They are your greatest asset, so don't under-invest in them—just believe.

5) Be willing to make the tough calls on people. All of the worst mistakes I have made as a leader have been waiting too long to make the tough call on someone who clearly was not going to be able to deliver in the role. You owe it to the rest of the team to be a leader and help these people move on quickly, not burdening the rest of the team with the work that is not getting done or the issues that will be created.

6) Be a leader in every way. Leadership gets defined too narrowly sometimes. I think we should be expansive in our definition. It involves everything you do: taking the time to coach a colleague when they clearly need it; being direct and honest when someone needs to hear it; providing the inspirational message when the group is demoralized; focusing the agenda when the work

seems overwhelming; getting the team out for some fun when people need a break. You are spectacular people. Allow yourselves to make a difference for the people around you.

7) Make your McKinsey experience extraordinary. Don't *take* projects or clients, *select* them. Don't work with people who aren't committed to you personally. Invest in building a set of clients and experiences you are interested in, and don't worry if that doesn't work out, you will land someplace great regardless. Take advantage of opportunities to see amazing places. Don't let anyone tell you what to do; just do what you love and do it well.

8) Always remember it is a really small world. Never burn bridges; never leave something unfinished; never dump something on someone else because you are upset and leaving; try not to "throw someone under the bus," even if they deserve it. The world you will inhabit in senior management is very small, and bad behavior is remembered long after you leave. (I think that was a Marc Anthony speech in *Julius Caesar*, but Shakespeare was a better writer). Doing the right thing will come back to you over time, so don't worry if it is not immediately recognized.

I wish you the best of luck in whatever you choose to do. Please stay in touch. I am always available to you (just call me. I will never be too busy to help if I can).
Chris

Despite some of the feelings and emotions I might have had about my partner review, I finished my last few weeks at McKinsey by helping win a new piece of work at a major gaming client I had served extensively. I coached a number of talented young people on how they could design a successful and energizing career path at the firm; and I sent out this note to a large group of people with the goal of inspiring and energizing them to live out their dreams and achieve their potential.

There were definitely moments where I wanted to brag about my great new job or talk about the blunt feedback I had received from the review committee, but I held back those feelings because they would have gotten in the way of my leaving on the best possible note.

More recently, during my last month at Kimberly-Clark, I invested incredible energy making sure to execute my tasks with excellence. I focused on making some important leadership changes that needed to be implemented, pushing forward the strategic business plan, helping the newly appointed leader with the transition process, and making sure all the key initiatives we were driving did not skip a beat.

This is the lesson I would leave with you: When you leave a company you leave a legacy, good or bad. If you let that legacy be defined by the anger you may feel about the circumstances of your departure, then you will likely leave a negative legacy that may very well come back to you in the future, and it is not worth it. You have one chance to leave a last impression. Make it a spectacular one.

CHAPTER 9

The 80/20 Rule

The 80/20 rule is the concept that 80 percent of the value in any analysis or evaluation is generated by the first 20 percent of the work. I am sure that most of us have heard this rule of thumb numerous times. It certainly has been mentioned many times during my career. My experience has been that the rule rings true more times than not. When you begin investigating any issue or idea, you start off learning very fast, and then the rate of incremental learning declines dramatically as the work progresses. This concept also seems to hold true with any agenda you may develop to improve the business. The top four or five ideas in a list of twenty-five always seem to drive 80 percent (or more) of the value.

I think this is an important rule to keep in mind as you progress in your career. We all want to be rigorous in exploring new ideas and options, but we also need to speed up decision-making and focus the team on the biggest ideas quickly, so that they can take action and create value.

The key is to strike the right balance, to find the right amount of depth to dig into any issue before you reach the point of diminishing marginal returns. If you rush a decision, you might miss something in your analysis and make the wrong decision, but if you over-analyze every decision, you will fail to take action, and your team and the business will suffer.

I have observed leaders who fall on both sides of the 80/20 demarcation line. There are quite a few people who get to an answer or draw a conclusion fast, and they feel very comfortable making a decision with only minimal analysis. I tend to fall into this camp. Once I have done a little analysis of an issue or idea and I have debated the pros and cons with a few capable colleagues, my bias is to encourage the team to make the decision and move forward fast. This can be a positive, as it creates a bias for action in the organization, but it can also have negative consequences. There is no doubt that I have overlooked some important risks and consequences as I considered options and made important decisions during the course of my career.

Other leaders prefer to analyze issues in great depth prior to making a decision. They will complete a rigorous analysis of a problem or decision, then debate the pros and cons of the issue with the team, then ask for more analysis to clarify key issues or concerns, then debate the issues and risks some more. In the end, it may take months to finally make a decision. On the plus side for this approach, these people tend to think very rigorously about their work and decisions. But they can also paralyze an organization and slow down decision-making to a standstill, killing the energy and enthusiasm of their teams.

I worked for a leader like this when I joined Guinness as the vice president of strategy for the Americas region. He was a very smart and capable leader, an ex-consultant who had been successful at another consumer products company before joining Guinness as president of the Americas division.

This leader was also an analytical animal. He loved to dig into detailed analyses and tear apart issues by building a massive fact base, analyzing every possible outcome or permutation. After he hired me, I remember a conversation where he brought up the 80/20 rule. He encouraged me to push well beyond the first 20 percent of the work analysis and not to settle for getting things directionally correct. He wanted me to get to 95 percent or more of the answer by grinding through the data and the information in tremendous detail.

His thinking was that this would allow him (as the operating leader) to be more comfortable operating at 80/20 because he would know that my team had taken the analysis to such great depths. The problem with his logic was that he was not an 80/20 decision maker. His natural bias was to strive for the "perfect answer" on the big issues, regardless of how long it took to get there. He continued to demand more analysis and more detail around every decision, no matter what level of rigor my small strategic planning team had applied.

I remember one specific decision we had to make that involved shifting our brands and business out of our current distribution partner in our largest state and splitting it among a network of new distribution partners. As a team, we had debated the issue at length, and we all believed it was the right answer. We were clearly struggling with execution in this high-volume state, and we had been successful with similar moves in other states. But this was not sufficient for our leader.

He wanted to analyze the issue thoroughly before

making such an important decision. We gathered case examples from across the country. We evaluated market share and other performance trends in the covered distribution area. We determined the likely transition costs and potential volume loss due to the transition. And we interviewed industry experts to deepen our knowledge of the tradeoffs. Every piece of data we uncovered continued to support the decision to change our distribution strategy.

The analytical rigor we invested in this decision-making process was exhausting for me. Given my tendency to make decisions fast, I was trying to push my boss to make the call now and move on to the implementation process, but I was also trying to find a good balance and heed his request to be more rigorous and demanding on the analysis, so that he could feel comfortable making what was clearly a difficult decision for him.

After months of work and numerous reviews, we had a final decision meeting at an offsite location. During the meeting, we laid out the key decision drivers and our assessment of each of them, an analysis of the potential risks and long-term potential benefits to the business, the team's recommended strategy, and the plan, with a timeline to implement that decision. Everyone in the room was aligned with the decision, with the exception of our boss.

Instead of driving the team to conclude the work and move forward, he began to identify additional analyses we should probably complete before we finalized the work. At that point, I lost my cool. I challenged him in front of the team, reiterating all of the work that had been completed and the clear evidence that the decision was the right one, and I then emphasized the need to make the decision and move forward. I was so hungry to stop analyzing the issue and take action that I just could not hold back any longer.

At the next break, my boss called me aside and lit into me. He was furious that I had challenged him in front of the team and undermined his position. I tried to explain that I was simply trying to drive us to a decision and that I felt we had evaluated the issue sufficiently such that any further analysis was unnecessary. However, he was adamant that I had gone too far and that I should not publically challenge his authority in the future. He believed that he was trying to get the operating leaders to step up and argue for the decision, and he did not see it as my role to do that for them.

As you can imagine, this was a tough moment. I did not want to have an angry confrontation with my boss, but I also did not want to see us delay making a decision that was important to the business. As I look back now, it is clear that the real confrontation was between two very different styles. He was a highly analytical leader who was willing to go well beyond 80/20 in order to make sure his decisions were correct. I was the opposite. I tried to do the minimum amount of analysis necessary to validate a decision, and then I preferred to put that information in front of the team to drive a debate and a decision. My operating hypothesis has always been that it is better to take action sooner, fix any mistakes along the way, and maintain organizational momentum and energy.

Despite our differences, we each had something to learn from each other. I needed to be willing to build a stronger fact base for the most important decisions; he needed to know when to draw the line and cut off further analysis so that the team could make a decision and take action. Both of our styles had strengths and weaknesses, but because neither of us was willing or able to adjust our style at that moment, we could not find a constructive way to work together.

I have struggled with finding the right balance between rapid decision-making and rigorous analysis throughout my career. My bias remains the same: I prefer to develop clear hypotheses regarding the likely answers up front, focus the team on a clear and simple set of analyses, and then force a debate among capable leaders to drive a decision and action. In general, I believe that this is the right approach. Leaders need to have a bias for action to maintain organizational pace and momentum. But I have been party to situations where leaders' biases for action got them in trouble as well.

When I was a partner at McKinsey, I served a CEO of a midsized company who had a huge bias for action. He was a street-smart leader who had worked his way up from the bottom of the company, but he lacked some of the analytical and financial skills that you might expect of a leader in his position. However, what this leader lacked in analytical skills, he made up for in raw instinct for the business.

He had thirty years of experience at the company at all levels, and he knew the business, the operating challenges, and the competition very well. He used these instincts and his collaborative relationship with the trusted colleagues on his team to quickly evaluate issues and opportunities and make decisions fast. This allowed the company to react and adapt quickly to competitive activity and market shifts. The company copied competitive products, aggressively reacted to pricing changes, and moved quickly into new segments in a manner their less nimble competitors simply could not match.

The management team's bias for action and comfort with limited analytical rigor allowed them to outmaneuver and frustrate their competitors for years. But then they finally ran into a situation where the failure to fully evaluate an opportunity got the team and the company into trouble. They made a large acquisition without fully assessing the challenges and obstacles to integrating the business. They made this decision with no outside help and only a short period to assess the transaction. But once the deal closed, they found all sorts of problems:

- Plant assets were old and unreliable and would require a huge capital investment to bring them up to date.
- The accounting for sales and the discounts applied were not consistently rigorous, and they were forced to take large write-downs through the balance sheet.
- The customer base was eroding faster than they had estimated.
- Integrating the IT infrastructure was going to be much more difficult and expensive than originally estimated.
- The product and intellectual property pipeline was substantially less attractive than had been assumed in the investment thesis.
- The sheer size of this acquisition was much bigger than their previous experience, and the time and effort it took to integrate it proved to be a major distraction to both management teams, causing the business to suffer.

These setbacks and issues combined to make the acquisition much less attractive than had been estimated originally, and it meant the company had substantially overpaid for the acquired business. As the board began to dig into these issues in the post-acquisition analysis, it was clear that the management team had failed to complete a rigorous review of the potential acquisition target and that many of these issues should have been discovered during the due diligence process. That failure to apply a rigorous enough review eventually cost an otherwise capable CEO his job.

The key learning for me in all of this is that each of us has to find the right 80/20 balance that works for us, and we will likely need to apply that formula in a case-dependent manner.

The first step is to recognize your bias. Are you the type of leader who leaps to a decision with a minimal amount of analysis? Or are you the type of leader who tends to over-analyze an issue and fails to make a decision in a timely manner? Each of us has to be aware of our bias and then work to find the right balance in our decision making process.

- If you tend to jump to the answer too quickly, you may want to consider adding a few leaders to your team who are more analytically rigorous than yourself, or share your work with colleagues who are more rigorous and get their feedback. Furthermore, you will need to be open to a process that provides sufficient time for those leaders to complete a thorough review of the issues before making the final decision. Do not lose your bias for action, as it will help the team maintain positive

momentum, but be open to taking more time to deliberate on issues that are of critical importance to the business
- If you tend to agonize over decisions and demand a very high level of analytical rigor from your team before reaching a conclusion, you may need to consider adding a couple of leaders with a strong bias for action to your team, or share your work with teammates with this bias and ask them to challenge you to simplify and accelerate the approach. And you will need to work hard to integrate their thinking with your own and be open when they challenge you to make the decision faster. In addition, you will need to work hard to segment your decisions, allowing some decisions of lesser importance to be resolved very quickly through debate and other more important decisions to go through a more rigorous review process.

Getting to the right balance will require you to be self-aware and to be willing to adapt your working style based upon the nature of the decision. There will be times when a bias for action will help the team resolve issues quickly and maintain organizational momentum; and there will be other times when greater analysis is required, because the decision is of great importance and the answer is complex. It is up to you to assess what the circumstances demand and adjust your style and the process accordingly. The best place to start is to have an open dialogue with your team and teammates about your respective styles and how best to work together as a team to deliver on your goals and objectives. This will help create transparency on the team about the natural bias you all bring to problem-solving and decision-making and allow the team to work together on creating the right balance.

One final warning I would offer is to avoid the mindset or mentality that as you get more senior, your team (and your colleagues) should adjust to your style, rather than you adjusting to theirs. This is an arrogant mindset that is easy to fall into as you attain more success and more influence in an organization. Regardless of our positions, we all need to know our natural tendencies and be willing to adjust our styles based upon the situation.

For myself, I know that I tend to make decisions too quickly at times, so it is my responsibility to include more analytical thinkers on my team and to integrate their thinking into my own. This will allow for a greater diversity of thought on my team and inspire us to make better decisions over time. This is important because the goal should be to find the best answer for the company and the best outcome for shareholders, not just the best answer I happen to come up with. If achieving this outcome requires me to adapt my style based upon the circumstances, then I will do it. I cannot let hubris get in the way of delivering the best result for the many stakeholders we serve.

CHAPTER 10

Transparency Changes Everything

Very few people are completely transparent. There are plenty of people who are honest but very few who are genuinely transparent. This may sound contradictory, but allow me to define transparency before you pass judgment. Real transparency means that absolutely nothing is hidden or held back and everything is shared in an open and honest way.

That definition implies that you do not hold back on any question, any feedback, any information, any feelings or emotions, any concerns, or any excitement or passion you may feel for an issue or topic. Everything you think and feel is on the table all of the time, without compromising confidences.

Sharing that way with others takes great self-confidence and maturity because you cannot predict how others might react in a given situation, and you lose some perceived control of your ability to manage each situation. I have found, however, that this level of openness changes the game in terms of a leader's personal impact on his or her team. This is because transparency builds trust, and real trust allows great teams to function at a higher level.

Transparency does not mean that you unload on people and let every raw emotion flow forth in a tirade or rant, but it does imply that you share everything you feel and think in the moment. This can be done in a positive way, by complimenting a courageous or innovative idea, followed by expressing the concerns you may have regarding it or sharing your hopes and dreams for a person but then pointing out some of the issues that may hold the individual back from reaching that potential.

Complete transparency does not mean that there is no filter between your brain and your mouth. In fact, you may have to work hard to find the right words to share your reactions transparently but in a manner that does not discourage others. Transparency simply means that you never conceal an idea, issue, or concern that is in your mind and needs to be heard.

In my experience, very few people are this open and transparent with the professionals with whom they work. People tend to hold back and only share certain emotions, select information, and specific details about their opinions or feelings regarding any issue. They are not being dishonest by holding back these feelings or details. They are choosing to withhold reactions, concerns, and opinions that they may hold on a topic or issue, usually for fear of hurting another person's feelings or eliciting a negative reaction.

I understand why people hold back. They are worried about sharing too much or about sending the wrong message and leaving a bad impression. But I think they are making a mistake, because complete transparency builds a deep and enduring trust that changes the way people work and relate to them. When a colleague knows he or she will always get a straight and honest response from a leader, no matter how difficult the topic, it changes everything. It unlocks an unguarded discussion that allows for real problem solving and collaboration.

I have always considered myself to be open and honest with my teams and colleagues. But early in my career, that was not always true. I wanted to be liked and to impress people, and that desire led me to hold back and manage the message in a manner that was less than fully transparent. I can remember a number of examples, but one situation that stands out for me occurred during my brief time at CSC Index consulting in Chicago. When I joined, I was given the task of helping to build an analyst program at the firm, and we quickly attracted five or six talented young people from a mix of backgrounds who could help add analytical depth to our client work.

Analysts were a new phenomenon at CSC, and there was a lingering perception that the reengineering work we were leading with clients required more senior individuals with more experience and maturity. As a result, we worked hard to hire a mix of backgrounds: some with two to three years of experience and some right out of school, but with a very high bar for performance and maturity.

The aim was that the program would be well-regarded and leveraged by the leadership group in the company. Luckily, we were able to build a very talented initial team and provide team members with just enough training that they were performing well on their consulting teams, adding value to their clients, and creating immediate demand pull for analysts across the firm.

It was a great start for the program, and the team that was responsible for it was obviously protective of the reputation they were building within the firm. That reputation led to our facing a tough choice when we were asked to consider promoting a talented person from the graphics department into the analyst program.

The issue was not with her—she was a very smart and capable person; the issue was whether this would send the right signal to the rest of the organization about the type of talent that was being recruited to the analyst program.

The head of the Chicago office wanted us to promote this individual to show that the firm recognized the talent and contributions of everyone at the firm, including the non-client-facing teams. However, the analyst team was justifiably concerned that promoting her into the program might diminish the perception of our team at a time when we were still building momentum.

It was a difficult choice, and I tried to bring the team into it and make team members feel like part of the final decision, but I was not fully transparent with them. I asked them to consider the pros and cons and give me their feedback, but I was not completely transparent about how strongly the Chicago office leader was pushing for this promotion or that I had committed to him that I would seriously consider it.

Instead, I tried to make everybody happy. To the team, I put the issue on the table as one that was undecided, but to the office leader, I showed real excitement about the idea and told him I was supporting it with the analyst team. I was honest with all of them, but I was not fully transparent. I remember one particular meeting where one of the most talented and insightful analysts looked at me and asked, "Has this decision already been made, and are you just trying to make us feel better about it?"

I do not remember my exact response, but I know that I indicated that the decision was not final and that I wanted them to debate the issue and give me their recommendation. That was true, but it failed to reflect how strongly my boss was pushing for us to support the promotion.

As I think back on this from the leadership perspective I have today, I know that I would handle this debate very differently. To begin with, I would bring all stakeholders together to discuss and debate the issue face to face. I would sit down with the office leader and the team at the same time, lay out the pros and cons of the decision, and let them debate it openly, without acting as a middleman.

If the debate became contentious, I would step in and try to help each side see the other's perspective. And at the end of the debate, I would require a decision, regardless of whether it was by democratic vote of the team or by fiat, as a decision made by either the office leader or me. I would force the decision to be made in that room and in front of everyone.

That would have been the fully transparent way to handle the decision. Instead of going back and forth between the office leader and the team and hoping to make everyone happy, I would have simply let the debate happen and trusted that we would get to the best answer together. It probably feels risky to some, because you cannot completely control the open debate or the outcome, but it would have built real trust.

Everyone would have known that I was listening and open to both sides of the issue and that I was willing to hear everyone's input to the debate prior to making the final decision. As a leader, you have to trust that opening up the debate like this will get to the best outcome, and if you believe in your team, that is really not such a big risk.

I put myself in these difficult situations many times in my early career. I was always working to make everyone happy, and in the process, I found myself constantly trying to "sell" people on an outcome. It was stressful for me, it was draining, and it was not fully transparent.

I remember another situation at Guinness/United Distillers when I was running the Latin America region. I was working with our partner in Panama to launch a product called XLR8. It was an alcoholic soft-drink product that was targeted at a younger consumer segment. It had first been launched in Australia, and the segment later became popular in the United States.

The partner in Panama took the younger positioning to the extreme and created a series of commercials that targeted very young club-goers, so youthful in appearance and style that it was easy to see how this might be appealing to consumers below the legal drinking age. When my boss at Guinness saw the planned advertising, he was naturally concerned. Guinness/United Distillers was a multinational company that was very concerned about its brands and image, and he did not want to risk overtly recruiting consumers below the legal drinking age.

On the other side, I had the partner, who was investing in a risky new category idea and trying to stand out in a crowded market. Once again, I found myself caught in the middle. I did not want to anger my boss and create risk for the company, but I also wanted my regional partner to be excited about the opportunity and to invest in this new category concept.

Here again, I focused too much on making everyone happy and not enough on creating a truly transparent dialogue about the issue. I remember having conversations with our local partner in which I raised the issue about the target demographic, but I was reluctant to be too critical for fear of curbing his enthusiasm. I also remember having conversations with my boss where I agreed with his concern regarding the advertising and I committed to working with the partner to rework the creative and refocus on a slightly older consumer segment.

I was honest with both parties, but I never brought them together to discuss the issues in a genuinely transparent way in order to find a real compromise. I wanted to control the dialogue, and I was worried that my boss might anger the local partner. I was equally worried that the local partner might simply tell my boss that he was proceeding with the product launch regardless of the feedback from Guinness. I worked hard to try to make both parties happy, but it felt like I was caught in the middle and having to sell each party on the ideas and concerns of the other.

Once again, the fully transparent way of handling this would have been to force the discussion and debate. I should have brought both sides together, whether on the phone or in person, and I should have explained the issues and the challenges each side faced, forcing the tough discussion. I would not have been able to control what my boss said or what the partner said, but I should have trusted that the team would reach a compromise through an open and honest discussion, and that I could help the team reach that discussion by listening intently to team members' respective positions and helping them frame both the challenge and the opportunity. But instead, I tried to manage both sides to an outcome, and, in the process, I had to "sell" each on the other's position. It was stressful, it was unproductive, and it was not truly transparent.

This has been a key learning for me as I have progressed through my career: there is a difference between honesty and transparency. Genuine transparency changes the game. When I finally learned to let go of my desire to please everyone and control every situation, I focused on just letting the heartfelt debate rage so that the core issues and concerns could be exposed, it created a level of trust with my colleagues and teams that I had never experienced before.

I have found this also is true when it comes to offering feedback to people. Early in my career, I tended to sugarcoat the feedback I offered my team members. I told them the truth, but I tried to emphasize the positive aspects in order to make the feedback easier to swallow. I was not trying to deceive anyone, but I was reluctant to hurt a team member's feelings, and I did not want to have to deal with a potential negative response or reaction.

However, I have learned over time that this is unfair to the person to whom you are offering the feedback, and it simply delays the inevitable discussion that needs to happen. Today when I am asked for straight feedback, I provide it without hesitation. I am not mean about it, but I never withhold information that I think is critical for the person to hear.

I recently had a situation where a very senior leader on my team asked about his upside career potential beyond the vice president level he had already achieved. I told him that he was doing fine in his current role, but that he was unlikely to be considered for more senior positions at the company, based on his capabilities and performance trajectory. This was tough feedback for him to hear, as he had been with the company a long time, and he wanted to keep moving up. But it was the right feedback for him to hear, because the senior leadership team had specifically discussed his situation at our previous senior leader calibration meeting, and we had all reached this conclusion together.

It turned out that the reason this leader was asking these questions of me was that he was considering a more senior position at another company. In the end, he chose to leave and join that company based upon the discussion I had with him. If I had held back and simply told him that he was doing fine in his current job and that we would evaluate him for other positions as they came up in the future, that would have been an honest assessment, but not a fully transparent one.

The fully transparent discussion allowed him to make the best decision for himself based on a complete understanding of his situation at the company. It may not have been the answer he was looking for, but it was genuine, and he thanked me for being so straight with him after he had announced his decision to leave. In addition, his decision to leave allowed me to reorganize his department and promote some of the terrific talent that was coming up in the organization. I did not plan on making these changes, but the sudden departure of the leader allowed us to take a fresh look at how best to organize for success going forward.

The big insight that I have realized over many years

is simply this: Complete transparency changes the game. It builds genuine trust, and it allows the right issues and concerns to get out in the open so that the team can problem-solve them in a meaningful way.

Being this transparent can be scary because you cannot control how any situation may transpire. You cannot control the debate, you cannot control how others will react, and you cannot completely control the outcome. But you can control how you behave and lead. You can be direct and honest, and you can do that in a manner that is both positive and fully transparent—and that builds lasting trust.

I cannot emphasize enough how big a difference this can make for you as a leader. When your colleagues and teams genuinely trust you and believe in you, they will do anything for you. They will help you through any challenge, they will invest any amount of time necessary, and they will share their ideas and insights openly and passionately. They will be there when you need them, but you have to earn this level of trust and commitment. The best way to earn it is to start by being completely transparent with them, no matter how difficult the topic or situation may be.

CHAPTER 11

On Greed and Gravitas

Money can be a dirty subject. It is part of every job, and compensation is a key function within every company, but it is a topic that nobody really likes to talk about openly. As a result, negotiating compensation can be a delicate endeavor. You want to make sure that your compensation is consistent with your market value, but you do not want to push so hard that you will leave a bad impression with the people with whom you are negotiating.

I have been through numerous compensation negotiations, both as the employee and the employer, and I have seen both ends of the spectrum. Some people push way too hard and look greedy or non-committal; other people do not push hard enough, and you wonder why they accepted the first offer and whether they are tough enough; and a few people manage to get it just right. Regardless of the final outcome, how you manage these negotiations will leave a lasting impression, so it is worthy of careful consideration and preparation.

I did not have the opportunity to negotiate my first job offer at all. Boston Consulting Group had a standard offer for college graduates joining their analyst program, and it was non-negotiable. So my first opportunity came when I joined NutraSweet about three years later. I do not remember all of the details of twenty-five years ago, but I was offered the position of manager, strategy and capital analysis, reporting to the vice president of finance for the sweetener business. I had no MBA, but I had three years of strategy consulting experience and plenty of ambition.

I wish I could remember the actual salary numbers, but I remember having no conception of market pay for the position and no real logic for my negotiation strategy. The company simply made an offer, and I asked for 15 percent more. We settled in the middle. I would not call it a well-thought-out negotiation, but I figured I should not accept the first offer I was given. I would probably not recommend this as a best practice approach, but it was somewhat effective, and I do not remember my new boss seeming to feel that I pushed too hard.

The next compensation discussion of which I have a detailed memory was with Guinness/United Distillers. I was offered the role of vice president of strategy for the Americas. It was late 1994, and I was just turning thirty years old. I remember that I aggressively negotiated my salary and sign-on bonus for this role, and the primary logic I used was the cost of living difference associated with moving to the Northeastern United States from Chicago.

After visiting the area and looking at houses with my wife, I calculated the incremental costs we would face in terms of housing, taxes, and general cost of living, as well as the pay raise I thought was appropriate as I jumped to the vice-president level. I used that data to challenge the sign-on bonus, the housing allowance, and the base salary.

It was a data-driven negotiation technique, and I think it was reasonably effective. A number of new hires have used the same strategy on me when they joined my team. As long as the data are accurate and reasonable, I think it is a strong basis for a negotiation position.

The most difficult and contentious negotiation I went through was with Whitlock Packaging Corporation. As I was considering joining the company as president and CEO, I found that it was relatively easy to reach agreement on base salary and bonus for the position, but negotiating the equity part of the compensation was very challenging. The principal owner was the entrepreneur who had founded the company, and he obviously took great pride in his company. Like most founders of companies, he also was prone to overestimating what the company was worth. As a result, we went back and forth on current value and the equity stake I should expect if we were successful in growing the value and then selling the company.

These can be very tough negotiations because the value of the company is so very personal to the founder. In arguing for a lower initial valuation, I was in the uncomfortable position of having to argue that his "baby" was actually worth less than he believed. I used the earnings history and market EBITDA multiples to make the conversations more data-driven, but it was still very emotional. We eventually settled on a value and an equity agreement. Ultimately, I left the company before it was sold.

This highlights another important learning area for me: when the equity portion of your compensation is an important part of the total, you need to be clearly aligned with the people who control the equity on a likely exit strategy. I thought I had secured this alignment, but I was wrong. Looking back, I can see that the warning signs were clear, based on the time it took to align on an initial valuation. The founder had a strong emotional attachment to his business, and despite his stated goal of selling the company, I should have recognized that we might never achieve a valuation for the business that would be enough to meet his expectations.

Another instructive salary negotiation was the one I engaged in with Kimberly-Clark as I accepted the role of chief strategy officer. I pushed for a higher up-front salary based on market data and the salary of the previous executive who held the position. However, I made a point of not being too aggressive with my demands. At very senior levels, I think it is inappropriate to negotiate too hard. It simply sends the wrong message about your level of commitment to the company and your desire to be a leader there.

The reality is that these jobs all pay extremely well. Most of the compensation for these high-level jobs is set by market comps, and the executive incentive plans are established with the involvement of the board of directors. There is not that much flexibility other than with housing allowances, sign-on bonuses, and initial equity grants. Since I was not moving and I was not leaving behind any unvested equity at my previous employer, I had little basis for an aggressive negotiation.

I have seen other senior executives approach compensation and contract negotiations very aggressively, and I think it sends the wrong message. I remember one executive who was hired into a very senior role at one of my client companies while I was at McKinsey. The executive brought two lawyers to his contract negotiation. They challenged everything, including salary, sign-on bonus, equity grants, the severance agreement, and the change of control provisions.

I remember that the company lawyers felt that they had been put through the ringer when the employment contract was finally completed. This left a very bad impression on company leadership. It made them think that the new executive was out for himself, rather than the company. Although he did end up joining the company and doing well for a couple of years, he was abruptly pushed out for some questionable behavior. I do not know if it had anything to do with his negotiation approach, but I am certain that everyone loved watching him fall from grace. There were many in the company who had taken an immediate dislike to his self-serving style, and they were rooting against him during his entire tenure.

Since my initial negotiation with Kimberly-Clark, I have not challenged any offer at all. I may ask to clarify a few details in the employment contract, but I feel that it is unseemly to push aggressively for more compensation when the offer is already quite high. I think that it is acceptable to ask to see market data to evaluate where the offer stands versus comparable positions at benchmark companies, but as long as the data indicate that the offer is reasonable, I would be reluctant to push aggressively for a more attractive contract.

The relationships you forge up front with the board of directors and the senior executive team are too important to compromise based upon the desire to add 5 or 10 percent to an already substantial pay package.

Given my twenty-eight years of experience negotiating

compensation at eight different companies, on both sides of the negotiating table, my recommendations for any person negotiating an employment offer or contract would be the following:

1) **Always negotiate.** During your early- to mid-career, if you have the opportunity to push for a better deal, you should. If you take the first offer given, it suggests that you may not fight hard for what you believe in. So I would never accept the first offer provided early in your career. There is always some flexibility and the expectation that you will have some unique needs or demands. Take advantage of that expectation and try to make reasonable demands to increase the offer.

2) **Be data-driven.** Try to provide reliable data about other offers you are considering, the cost of living impact you will face, the comparable salaries at competing companies, or other data relevant to the potential offer.

   It is always advisable to negotiate using hard facts to back up your demands. It can help demonstrate that you are an analytical thinker who is capable of building a compelling argument and then negotiating effectively on your own behalf. It may take some time and energy to complete your research, but it is worth the investment.

3) **Do not get emotional.** Negotiating compensation can be emotional for some people. They get their feelings about their self-worth and value tied up in the discussions, and it can lead to an inappropriate response in the heat of the moment. Do your best to keep your emotions in check.

Write down a list of your demands and expectations. Make sure you reference the data you have collected to support those demands, and then let the hiring manager respond. He or she may challenge some of your requests or have conflicting data for you to consider, but you cannot let your emotions get in the way of always maintaining an even keel as you conduct negotiations with a potential employer.

4) **Know when to back off and seek a compromise.** It is important to stay alert and listen to the other side as you manage the negotiation. This typically allows you to discover where they have flexibility to negotiate and where they do not. I have dealt with candidates who keep pushing for something that I have already said is not negotiable, and it can be extremely irritating. As the representative of the company, your goal is to attract the new hire and make him or her excited about joining, but you also have limits in terms of what you can offer and still stay within the company salary structure.

Candidates need to listen for these limits as they negotiate and be nimble enough to accept certain terms while pushing for more in other areas where there may be more flexibility.

5) **Do not let the negotiation drag on.** Nobody likes to deal with a candidate who repeatedly asks for more. It is best practice to think through the entire offer carefully and identify the key areas you want to negotiate and why. Lay all of the facts and demands on the table up front and then push to get resolution within a couple of discussions.

So, take your time prior to the first call and gather a complete list of demands and a rationale for each. Put them all on the table, and use that first meeting to assess where the company negotiator has flexibility and where he or she may be hamstrung. Quickly accept the terms you can while challenging the ones that are important to you.

6) **Always be thankful.** Each time the company adjusts its offer in response to a request, thank the manager for the change and the flexibility, and attempt to show an equal amount of flexibility on another demand that may be less important to you. And at the end of the negotiation, remember to thank the hiring manager for the time he or she invested to help get your offer right and reinforce how excited you are to be joining the company. I have gone so far as sending a gift to the hiring manager at the conclusion of the negotiation, with a personal note thanking him or her for the effort put in on my behalf. Each time I have done it, the gesture has been very well-received.

7) **Be cognizant of the first impression you are creating.** You do not want to start your new job working for a manager you just angered during the negotiation process. You need to be sensitive to how you conduct yourself and what impact your conduct is having on the relationship with your potential new boss. If it is clear that the new boss is at the monetary limit, then you have to make a choice. Are you willing to accept the offer even though it may be below your expectations,

or would you rather pursue an offer with another company?

Be careful not to force an ultimatum. I think it is unwise to threaten that if the company cannot adjust to your demands you will go somewhere else. An ultimatum has the potential to create some enduring animosity. It is better to make your decision, and either accept the offer or try your luck elsewhere.

8) **As you get more senior, negotiate less.** This may seem counter-intuitive, as you may feel that you have more leverage and more options as you achieve more seniority. However, it is more important to show excitement about the opportunity and a commitment to being part of the team. The senior executive positions at most companies pay extremely well, and it can look greedy and self-serving to come in aggressively pursuing a more attractive compensation package.

I think it is acceptable to ask the company to share the market data they used to develop the offer and the executive compensation structure the board has approved for the leadership team. If the offer you receive seems inconsistent with this information, it may provide the basis for a negotiation. But if the compensation package is in line with market data and the approved company executive plan, then I would be reluctant to push aggressively for more. The risk of creating a negative initial impression with the board of directors and your new colleagues on the executive team is simply not worth it.

Negotiating compensation effectively is an art and not a science. Getting it right will require you to strike a delicate balance. You should expect to be compensated consistent with the market and your capability, and you should be willing to negotiate aggressively to achieve this goal. At the same time, you need to be cautious not to create a negative first impression with the people who will help you develop and progress in your career with the company.

In the end, the best advice I can give is to prepare in advance, listen carefully to the other side as the negotiation progresses, look for opportunities to compromise and find agreement wherever you can, and always keep in mind that you need to work with these people when the negotiation is over.

Do not read my caution the wrong way. Everyone deserves to be compensated in a manner that fully reflects their experience, skill, and future potential, but we also need our future employer to be just as excited about landing us after the negotiation as they were prior to the negotiation. So consider your approach carefully, and be sensitive to how your demands are being received by your future employer. As long as you maintain a balanced approach and make fair demands based upon market data, you are sure to accomplish the best outcome for yourself and the company.

CHAPTER 12

The Do-Nothing Strategy

Doing nothing is a strategy. It is a choice to maintain the current course or action plan, regardless of how the surrounding environment might have changed. This description may seem like an unfair characterization of a decision to stay focused on the current strategy, but I selected that name to make a point.

Nobody ever sits in a meeting to debate big new ideas and then concludes the discussion by stating that they have agreed to *do nothing*. However, the truth of the matter is that deciding to stick with the current strategy is, in fact, a decision not to make any substantial changes, which is precisely the do-nothing strategy. That strategy might be the right decision at any given moment, but it is not always the right decision.

My observation is that leadership teams are frequently incapable of breaking free from the gravitational pull of the current state. In my view, leaders often fool themselves into believing that maintaining the current course is fundamentally safer than any potential change of direction. They evaluate every new idea or plan against the value that they estimate will be created by the current strategy, often referred to as the base case. When they complete this analysis, they inevitably overestimate the value of the base case, and they risk-adjust every new strategy or idea to such an extent that it almost always looks less attractive than staying the course.

I think there is a fundamental flaw in this thinking and approach. In my experience, leaders and companies end up proving to themselves that doing nothing, that is, maintaining the current strategy, is the right decision over and over again, regardless of how the world is changing around them. When the analysis is complete, any new strategy always seems to involve more risk and more downside than the current strategy, and this often leads to stagnation and paralysis in companies and organizations.

Perhaps the poster child for the do-nothing strategy is Kodak. For years, this company's leadership team managed to convince itself that throwing the company into digital photography and digital image management was riskier than maintaining their position as the leader in film-based photography. I am certain that they invested in these new technologies and models, but they never invested themselves fully into redefining the business model of the company.

In hindsight, that approach looks like pure stupidity and incompetence, but put yourself in their shoes about fifteen years ago. The company made a ton of money selling film, they had a dominant brand and market share, and the business was still growing. I believe that their peak year of film profitability was right around the turn of the millennium. These facts made it very difficult to change direction and potentially jeopardize that market-leading position by betting big on digital photography and digital image sharing.

As a user of simple digital cameras and then an early adopter of smart-phone photography, I could not understand how the executives at Kodak did not see that their core product and their business model were going to be rendered irrelevant in just a few short years. But clearly, the risk of cannibalizing their core business made it difficult for the leadership team to abandon the company's film business and pursue an uncertain digital future.

I am sure that the leadership team performed countless strategic market assessments about the time the core business really started to erode. I would bet that each analysis started with a base case that showed slow erosion of the film business over many years but continued to forecast enormous profitability from the traditional business as it declined, making the risk of "abandoning the core" seem huge when compared with the incremental opportunity that might be created by new business models the company might have invested in at that time.

If you could pull those analyses out of the closet and revisit them today, I would bet that all of them underestimated the speed of change in the core business that would hit the company just a few years later. In other words, they overestimated the base case. As soon as smartphones were introduced with excellent cameras built into them, the film business effectively fell off a cliff. The new reality was that most consumers had no reason to print their pictures anymore because they could easily share photos through e-mail, texts, Myspace, and Facebook.

Less than ten years after the launch of the first mass-market touch-screen smartphones, Kodak was bankrupt, and their imaging patents and assets were being sold off for an ignoble end to a once-proud company.

Another unfortunate example of the do-nothing strategy is BlackBerry. It dominated the smartphone business for many years and had a huge market share and market capitalization advantage over its competitors. When the iPhone launched in 2007, I am sure that BlackBerry was concerned, but I doubt that the company's leaders saw the end coming in less than a decade.

After the company began to lose share in the ensuing years, I would assume that its managers evaluated the option of abandoning their iconic keyboard phone, but I would also bet that when they estimated the risk of alienating their core customers, they saw a huge potential for value loss and made the decision to stay the course, regardless of the massive market shift to touch-screen phones that was going on in the market around them. In the end, they stuck with that decision for more than five years, and they wiped out 95 percent of the market value of the company in the process.

These are dramatic examples, but I have seen this story play out many times during my career. Every big company has a core business. The more profitable that core business is, the more the leaders at that company want to protect it and stay focused on it. As a result, most of the breakthrough strategies, the really innovative ideas, get discarded as too risky or too distracting, and the bias is always to stick with the current strategy—regardless of how the market environment might be changing. In the final analysis, the do-nothing strategy wins the debate 99 percent of the time.

During my career with McKinsey, I observed this

phenomenon with many of my clients. The gravitational pull of the core business always seemed to hold leadership teams back from real innovation and game-changing strategies. I remember serving one large alcoholic beverage company that engaged us to look at the growth of imports and micro-brewed beers and to help them understand how to compete in that fast-growing segment.

We pulled together all of the market trend data, interviewed consumers and restaurant customers to evaluate what was driving these trends, and completed case studies on the most successful brands in order to understand how they were driving growth.

It was a comprehensive analysis that indicated that the trend would likely continue for many years and create enormous value in the marketplace. But it also indicated that it would be very hard for the major U. S. brewers to participate substantially, because consumers desired authenticity in these new products, and they did not really believe that the big brewers were credible producers of highly differentiated brands and products.

It was an interesting conundrum. On the one hand, this was a fast-growing new business that was gaining share at a higher price point than the core market, which made the segment attractive. On the other hand, the leadership team was worried that succeeding in this emerging segment might require the formation of an independent subsidiary that was free to pursue more aggressive and distinctive products and marketing tactics. And leaders worried that this strategy might distract the team from executing on the core business.

When the senior leadership team completed its analysis of this new opportunity, the team decided that, rather than form a new subsidiary, it would instead launch a few smaller brands within the current corporate structure that targeted this segment. Not surprisingly, none of those brands was successful, as the consumer research had predicted right from the start.

The new brands lacked any claim to authenticity, and consumers quickly rejected them. In addition, when the volume did not emerge as planned, the sales and marketing teams at this large company quickly de-prioritized the new brands in order to refocus on the core business. As a result, most of these brands were off the market within a year.

Big companies make this mistake all of the time. They are so worried about losing momentum and cannibalizing the core that they kill every big new idea and opportunity that might develop in the organization. I refer to this as "leading from fear," because the team is building its strategy based on the fear of losing in the current business rather than on exploiting the opportunity to build a new business.

I understand why this happens. It is important to focus on the core and drive continuous improvement in the business. But it is also important to continuously reinvent the company and drive innovation in the business model. Reinvention creates energy, it inspires the team, and it sets the organization up for future growth. But finding the right balance between staying focused on the core and driving meaningful innovation is a very tough leadership challenge.

I have failed at both ends of this challenge. There have been times when I failed to maintain the appropriate level of focus on the core, and there have been times when I failed to challenge the team to innovate aggressively beyond the core. At Whitlock Packaging, I let the possibility of an industry roll-up strategy and the potential for an outside, private equity investment in the company distract the team away from the need to improve the core business. We had substantial talent deficiencies and operating issues that needed to be addressed first, and I should have been intensely focused on fixing these issues before we considered any ideas that were outside of the immediate operating challenges.

More recently, when I was leading the international business for Kimberly-Clark, I believe we made terrific progress improving the core marketing and operating performance of the business, but we fell short in terms of expanding the business into new categories and adjacencies that would drive future growth. We launched a cost-transformation project; we created strong linkages between the innovation organization and the local leadership teams (resulting in improved products in our key markets); and we upgraded our operating leadership in markets that were struggling.

These steps allowed us to improve our operating results and deliver on market expectations, but I was disappointed with how few breakthrough ideas were generated and tested across the business. With our highly autonomous local markets and strong local leadership model, we had a great opportunity to experiment with breakthrough innovation that would help us sustain our growth trajectory into the future. But all of our relatively small investments in these areas were cut as we focused intensely on delivering our calendar-year results.

It was easy to make these cuts in the moment. We were

facing strong negative financial headwinds as emerging market currencies turned against us, and we prioritized marketing investments and product upgrades in key markets over longer-term product or business model innovation. But if companies always choose to prioritize the core business and the short-term operating priorities, they will fail to develop future growth opportunities which will be required to sustain the business in the long term.

Overcoming the bias to maintain the status quo is hard because it is easy to argue (and support that argument with financial analysis) that the core business should remain the number-one priority and that everything else should take a backseat to improving current operating results.

There is no formula for avoiding the pull of the do-nothing strategy, but over the years I have developed a few techniques that I use to help find the right balance.

1) **Refuse to accept the overly optimistic base case.** Every base-case scenario I have seen developed is simply a forecast of current profitability extending many years into the future. It typically projects slow and steady annual growth, and it almost never predicts or includes any disruptive events or radical changes in market conditions.

    As a leader, you have to challenge the base-case analysis and make sure it is not a completely unrealistic forecast of the future. If the base case is too attractive, almost all potential new strategies and business models will compare unfavorably.

    My suggestion is that you have a tough conversation with the team about the base-case scenario and encourage team members to think about how the core business could change over time. I would also think about having a range of base-case scenarios that include more disruptive possibilities.

2) **Challenge your team to plan with a future-focused mindset.**

    Most corporate planning is done under the assumption that the current market conditions and constraints will remain in effect during the planning period. This drives teams to assume that the current state will remain basically unchanged and, not surprisingly, they tend not to develop any radical new ideas or plans.

    In order to push my teams to think creatively, I try to develop "what-if" scenarios about what the market might look like in five years, and I then ask the team to think through how our company will need to adapt to be successful in that future environment. This expanded timeframe usually pushes the team to think more aggressively about how the market will evolve, how our competitive position will change, and the strategies that will be required to win in that new marketplace.

3) **Support multiple low-risk investments.**

    Big strategic choices can be intimidating. They may involve substantial risk, and therefore they can be scary to make. If a new strategic direction or innovation becomes an all-or-nothing plan, it will almost always get shot down as too risky. My suggestion is to have a portfolio of potentially game-changing ideas in development at all times.

If you can find low-risk ways to test and incubate ideas, it "de-risks" the decision and allows the ideas and strategies to grow organically within the organization.

If an idea turns out to be very successful, you can then scale it up based upon the learnings and insights the team has developed. If an idea fails, focus on learning why it failed and spreading those insights across the leadership team so that team members can benefit from the failure.

4) **Budget a modest amount for longer-term investments and manage the performance of those investments aggressively.**

You need to commit a fixed amount of funding to the new strategies and business models the team would like to test. Without fixed funding, these projects will always get cut when the budget is tight.

However, there also must be clear accountability and performance management for the pilot projects that the team invests in. Otherwise, these pilots may go on forever, regardless of the results they deliver. Without clear accountability, the pilot projects have the potential to anger the operating leaders who are working hard to deliver results and fund these investments. As a result, I would make sure the pilot teams have clear goals and milestones and that these goals are reviewed with the operating leadership on a consistent basis, so that the portfolio of projects can be pruned or expanded as appropriate.

In the end, this all comes down to finding

creative ways to challenge the status quo. I would suggest that you start by having an open dialogue with your team about how the external market is evolving so that you can objectively assess the relevance of your business model in that changing environment. I believe the pace of change is accelerating, and therefore leadership teams need to hold a robust strategic dialogue on a consistent basis in order to ensure the company strategy remains current.

I would also encourage you to be aware of how the pull of the do-nothing strategy is affecting your team and whether it is consistently overwhelming new ideas and opportunities. If every strategy session and review meeting seems to deliver the same outcome—e.g., a decision to maintain the current agenda—then you may have a problem with the way your team is looking at and evaluating new ideas. This is more art than science, but simply being aware of the decision-making bias of your team and working with the team to inject a more strategic look at how the market is changing is a great first step in making sure that you do not fall victim to the powerful gravitational pull of the do-nothing strategy.

CHAPTER 13

The Why Always Comes Before the What

I am constantly talking to my teams about "the big *why*." For me, this is the big idea or reason you are working on something. What I find is that many of the teams I work with cannot even define the big *why* for their work or project. They schedule time on my calendar to take me through a project plan or a timeline, and they fail to tell me why I should even care about the work they are doing. They jump right into talking about the *what* all of the required actions steps, implementation milestones, and investments that must be made—but they neglect to enroll or engage me with the reason *why* we want to do all of this work.

So I always ask them to start by telling me their big *why* before they drop down into sharing the detail and the *what*. Why is this a big idea? How much value will it create for the company? How could we leverage the idea to change our competitive position? This is a discipline that gets lost in big companies, as projects just seem to roll on ad infinitum and nobody seems to ask questions like, "remind me, why are we doing this?"

One of the best videos I have seen on this topic was a TED Talks presentation by Simon Sinek in which he described in detail why the *why* really matters. (Google the video and watch it—it will be worth your time). I try to consistently leverage the concept of putting the *why* at the center of everything I do. No matter what the topic, whether it is a marketing plan, a new product launch, a business integration plan, an IT plan, or a change management plan, I always try to ask a series of big *why* questions:

- Why should the customer/consumer care?
    - Why will they pay us more money or buy more of our products as a result of this work?
- Why should the company invest in this?
    - What value will it create and how might it change the game?
- Why should this be a top priority for us?
    - Why would we invest resources in this prior to other opportunities?
- Why should I personally be excited about this opportunity?
    - What makes it fundamentally different and innovative?

I try to ask these questions in a non-threatening way as we begin the discussion. I do not want to demean what people are working on. The goal is to help the team develop a compelling vision for their project/initiative with a clear description of *why* it matters. In many cases, the team has a very big idea, but they jump right to the *what* (the detailed work that needs to be done), and they fail to express how much value can be created or the big *why* for the project.

I think in some cases the team is simply being

conservative or humble, not wanting to over-promise or over-promote their work. But this mindset is troublesome because it may undersell the potential of the project and it may fail to enroll and engage the key stakeholders that will be required to execute it.

I have hundreds of examples of "failing to put the *why* before the *what*," almost too many to choose from. But I thought I would start with one where I was part of the working team, and then I will provide a more recent example where I was a more senior leader trying to find the big *why* in all the work that was going on around me.

The first example occurred when I was running the Latin America region for Guinness. Toward the end of my tenure there, the parent company, Guinness/United Distillers, agreed to merge with Grand Metropolitan Corporation. They created a new name for the company—DIAGEO—and a new mission statement: "We make lips smile," which was supposed to define why the merger made strategic sense (one of the less compelling mission statements I have seen in my career).

The integration created huge value for the combined spirits business, but it was less clear whether there were any synergies between the beer business (Guinness), the fast food business (Burger King), and the ice cream business (Häagen-Dazs). These were all great brands and businesses, but it was unclear to me what value was going to be created by having them in the same portfolio. I was asked to serve on a team chartered to do just that for the Latin America region. Each business unit sent one representative to a series of meetings with the goal of finding synergies between these businesses in our region, and we jumped right into that task, meaning that we began working on the *what*.

However, it quickly became apparent that these were not synergistic businesses. They leveraged different distribution systems; they were radically different in terms of the sales and marketing strategy; and the geographic footprint was very diverse across the businesses. We found some opportunity to co-locate office locations, and there were some shared service synergies, but the value-creation opportunity was pretty limited overall.

After a number of weeks of working on this project and making very little progress, I remember talking openly with the rest of the team during a break in the meeting, and we came to a "big *why*" realization. The real value was probably not going to be created by integrating these diverse businesses; it was more likely going to be uncovered by selling them off to other natural owners who could get more value out of them.

It was a big insight that should have immediately changed the nature of the work we were doing, but it didn't. After the break, we went right back to the task of exploring whatever synergies we could find and summarizing that for senior leadership. We had been given an assignment and we were going to finish it no matter what.

In the end, DIAGEO ended up selling off all of these businesses, with the exception of the beer business. As the company leaders continued to invest in building their global spirits business, it must have become clear that these other businesses did not really fit, and they were better off in another company's portfolio. But at the time I was working on this project, the company was not ready to admit this reality, and the team I was part of was more than happy to start working on the *what* without taking the time to ask *why*.

This is a classic example. I have seen many projects and initiatives at big companies build up momentum and take on lives of their own to the point that the people doing the work stop asking *why*. The *why* gets lost, but the work goes on, and this creates waste because it allows low-value-added work to distract teams from bigger, better ideas with the potential to create real value.

The second example I will share with you occurred when I took over leadership of the Kimberly-Clark Professional (KCP) business. The business sold myriad products to other companies around the world, including towels, bath tissue, facial tissue, soap, sanitizer, industrial wipers, safety equipment, and other products that supported workplace environments. As I began to learn the business, I had the chance to visit plants, customers, innovation labs, distributors, and other facilities, and I quickly discovered a few things:

- Our product categories were commoditizing; margins were declining over time; and the value of our brand was not sufficient to differentiate our offering.
- The teams at KCP were working on a stream of innovation to upgrade products, but it was unclear whether those innovations would make much of a difference to end users.
- Most of the innovation pipeline consisted of marginal improvements to our current products, but there was no "big *why*" insight into customer needs that was driving the innovation, and nothing about the new product ideas that made me think that customers would pay more for them.

- Our marketing materials were bland and undifferentiated as well. There was no emotion to them at all—no real reason to buy—just product specs and a point-of-difference claim buried somewhere in the body of the text.
- Our sales teams were very proficient at selling products, describing product specifications, and negotiating prices, but they did not have a clear understanding of the unique value they offered their customers. They worked on preparing bids with distributors, and they did a great job of building and leveraging relationships, but it was unclear whether what they were offering was in any way different or better than the competition.

As I went through this learning process and talked at length with the team about what we were going to do about it, I happened to see the video by Simon Sinek I mentioned earlier, and I realized that we were all about the *what*, and we really had no clear understanding of our big *why*.

We sold products that were about the same as everyone else's in our industry; we were working on products that were about the same; our marketing materials looked about the same (or worse) than other suppliers; and we sold our products in about the same way as our competitors.

As a team, we were working very hard trying to improve margins with this undifferentiated bundle of "me too" products and services, but we had not defined what made us different from the competition, and we had no clear "big *why*" reason our customers should choose us.

As a result, we were struggling to make real progress. We were running in mud.

This was a big insight, because it forced us to step back and begin to frame what we wanted our "big *why*" to be and then use that as a guide to reframe the business model around this compelling reason for being. In the end, the team came up with the idea of "Exceptional Workplaces." They believed that what we should be about is helping companies create better workplaces for their people—healthier, safer, and more productive workplaces.

For me, that was a "big *why*" reason to get up and go to work every day, and it was an inspiring way for our salespeople to add value to the companies they served. From that point on, we set about redesigning our company, our marketing, our product bundles, and our sales process to deliver on the big *why* of Exceptional Workplaces. It was an exciting vision that galvanized the organization and led to transformational change.

The learning for me is that the *why* always has to come first. The *why* is the big vision, the big idea, or the big opportunity that has the potential to excite the people we work with and galvanize the team around a plan of action. Ideally, a big *why* captures and engages the heart as well as the mind, and it motivates people to fully commit to making something happen because they care. They become personally connected to the value proposition of the company or the project.

This realization has changed the way I lead in a fundamental way. As an ex-consultant I was all about the *what*. I could produce and present process charts, timelines, and Gantt charts as well as anyone, and I would always include an estimate of the potential value creation at the beginning and the end of the PowerPoint deck to ensure that there was a payback. But there was no emotion about it—no connection to the heart of the organization.

It was just a flow chart that said, "do step A first, then step B, then step C—add in some evidence that it will create economic value and that it worked at other companies—and then finish with a project structure chart with a steering committee at the top." I have seen hundreds of these decks, both as a consultant and as a senior leader, and when I look at them now they drive me crazy because, first, no project actually works that way, and second, they fail to engage the hearts and minds of the organization, and, as a result, they fail to fundamentally change anything.

The work simply becomes another project—nothing more—and it may add some short-term value, which is likely to be lost over time, but it does not fundamentally change the company or its strategic position. It does not add up to much in the end, even if there is a payback on the consulting fees required.

I go back to the presentation I saw Gary Hamel make regarding what he labeled the Hierarchy of Engagement. At the bottom of the hierarchy is compliance and diligence. This is what most companies get from their people, because they have created so much hierarchy, so many rules, and such structured processes that there is little intellectual freedom for the employee.

At the top of the hierarchy sits imagination, creativity, initiative, and passion. Great companies elicit these things from their people. They do it by engaging them in a big *why* vision for the company, a unique mission that has meaning to the marketplace and the organization, and they do it by creating freedom within the framework for people to take initiative and be entrepreneurial.

I want to lead and work for companies that engage people at that level. I want imagination, creativity, initiative, and passion from my teams, and I am not going to get that with a process chart and a few milestones. To engage a team this way, I have to start with an explanation of the big *why*—*why* the project or strategy matters and how it will fundamentally change things; *why* the team should care; *why* our customers should care; and *why* I care. When you engage an organization like this, you get much more from the team than compliance and diligence; you get genuine commitment and ownership. That is the difference between good and great.

CHAPTER 14

The Toughest Calls Are the Most Important

Over the years, I have asked scores of executives what their biggest mistake or regret was, and I consistently get the same answer: failing to move fast enough to make a change on the team when it was necessary to drive long-term success.

When they respond with this answer, the executives are typically not referring to the obvious decisions, those where someone is clearly failing to deliver or execute on their goals. For the most part, the executives are talking about the really tough calls, those instances when someone has done well in the past but seems to have been promoted beyond his or her capability; or the instance when someone just seems to have run out of energy and ideas after years of driving impact; or, even tougher, when someone is technically competent but does not seem to work well with the rest of the team.

Whatever the case, I agree with their assessments—the biggest mistakes you are likely to make as you progress in your career will be people mistakes—failing to make the tough calls on people and holding on to them for too long despite clear evidence that the team or the business is not performing up to its potential. These are the toughest decisions because you will not have perfect information, and there will always be a reason not to do it now. However, these decisions are also the most important ones you will make in your career.

My first real experience with this occurred when I moved down to Florida to assume leadership of the Latin America region for Guinness. It was a nascent business, and we had a very small team in place to support it. The three most important leaders on my direct team were the marketing manager and the two sales/relationship leaders for the region. Individually, they were all solid performers who were very committed to the business. We all lacked experience with the Guinness brand, but there was plenty of energy and enthusiasm and a real desire to learn.

But the team dynamic was dysfunctional. There was a lack of collaboration and lots of infighting, and the team was constantly coming to me to resolve the conflicts. As a young leader (I was thirty-one when I arrived in Florida), I assumed that resolving those conflicts was part of the job, but it got to the point that I was constantly playing peacemaker within the team.

The marketing manager possessed solid technical marketing skills, but she lacked self-confidence. When she presented materials to the sales leaders, and they gave negative feedback (they probably were not listening for the gold in those discussions), she tended to react in a defensive manner. She would then ask me to resolve the situation rather than attempting to resolve it directly. This approach eroded the trust between her and the two sales leaders, as they felt she was leveraging her proximity to me to force her ideas or her agenda on them. And I made the mistake of stepping into the middle of that argument over and over again.

I genuinely liked all three of the leaders involved in this dysfunctional relationship. They were good people who worked hard, but we were simply too small a team to tolerate this behavior. It slowed us down as a team and made us look like we were not aligned. I needed to make a tough call in order to get the team dynamic right, but instead, I continued to step in and attempt to barter the peace rather than insist that they change their behavior. I needed to hold them accountable for resolving their differences in a positive and expedient way and be willing to act if they failed to do that. But I never could muster the courage to do exactly that.

I spent almost three years in that job, and although the team dynamics improved to some extent, it never became a high-performing team. As I look back now, I realize I never made the tough call. I liked the people, and I wanted them to like me. Therefore, I tolerated the dysfunctional behavior in the team for years when I should have held them accountable within months of getting there. I kept telling myself that I would get them so excited about the vision and the potential for the team to win that they would put their differences aside and focus on the work. But it never happened, and we paid the price as a team because we failed to achieve the success we were capable of delivering.

I carried this learning into my next job as I moved to Tulsa to take on the role of president of Whitlock Packaging. Having just lived through this experience, I was determined to make the tough decisions faster in my next job. After a few months leading the company, I realized that our VP of operations was struggling. He was a smart executive with a terrific technical background, but he struggled as a senior leader. He had failed to build a consistently strong team; he was a weak communicator; he did not use a disciplined performance-management process to evaluate operating performance and provide feedback; and he struggled with the speed of his decision-making. I think I knew four to five months into the role that I had to make a change, but in the end it took me almost fourteen months to act.

As much as I was committed to making the tough people decisions faster, reasons or excuses kept popping up that slowed us down. We were worried that customers who were friendly with this leader might be angry. We were worried that some employees might be loyal to him and potentially leave with him. And we were worried that we did not have a backfill option ready to drop into the role. But these concerns were simply excuses. When we finally made the decision and asked him to leave, there was little or no negative response from customers or employees. I think I took one call from one concerned customer, but it did not affect our business at all. The customers and employees knew it was the right decision, as well.

I look back today, and my only regret is that I waited an additional nine months to make a decision that I knew would help the company. I thought I was holding off for the right reasons, but I should have made the decision faster and moved on. A faster decision would have accelerated our turnaround.

These decisions are so hard precisely because there always seems to be a good reason not to make the tough call. You might convince yourself that the person will respond with the right coaching, or you might convince yourself to wait until there is less potential for disruption, or you might convince yourself that it will take too long to find the right replacement. But these are all just excuses. In the end, if you know someone is simply not the right leader for the team, then you owe it to your team and yourself to make the tough call; so make it fast and move on.

Every leader struggles with this decision throughout his or her career. As a partner at McKinsey, almost every CEO or president I worked with had at least one direct report who was struggling and needed to be replaced, but in many cases the executive failed to make the tough call and delayed making the decision for years. I remember working with the CEO of a mid-sized retailer who had key senior leaders on his team who needed to be replaced, but the decision was so painful for him that he could not take action. The first leader, the CFO, had been working with him for more than twenty years, and although it was clear he was no longer driving change, the CEO just could not make the decision to accelerate his departure and get a more aggressive leader into that critical role.

In addition, one of the division presidents was a leader who had worked his way up from the bottom of the company, and the CEO loved him for that. However, the business had outgrown his capabilities, and he was clearly struggling to run the business at a more mature phase in its development cycle. Once again, it seemed like the CEO knew that he needed to make a change and put new leadership in this position, but nothing happened.

Everybody on the senior leadership team believed that these leaders needed to leave the company and that new energy and new ideas had to be injected into the business at a time when results were stalling, but the CEO could not make those tough decisions. It was simply too painful to think about asking such trusted long-term colleagues to leave the company, even if the business was suffering under their leadership. The CEO continued to delay making these decisions until a private equity firm finally acquired the company and made the decisions for him.

You will face the same challenges in your career. You will have leaders on your team who are technically competent and hardworking, and yet it will be clear to you and those around you that you need to make a change—a tough call. If you fail to make the tough decisions—if you fail to take action when you need to—the team will probably struggle, and you will likely fail to achieve your potential as a leader. These will be the hardest decisions you will make in your career, but they will also be the most important.

If you find yourself wondering about a leader on your team—thinking that maybe a change is necessary but you are just not sure—then I would recommend the following:

- First, ask yourself if the leader in question told you tomorrow that he was leaving, would you be disappointed about losing him or excited about the opportunity to recruit new talent to your team?
    - If the answer is that you would be excited to recruit new talent, then you probably have a tough decision to make, and if you fail to make it, you may be letting down the company and the people that work for this individual.
- Second, be really clear with the individual about your expectations for performance. Take the time

to write down what exceptional performance looks like—not acceptable performance, exceptional performance. Then share those very specific expectations with the individual.
  - Be very clear about the leadership behaviors you are looking for and the results you expect, and see how the struggling team member responds. If he gives you excuses about why those expectations are unrealistic, then you need to reiterate why nothing less than exceptional is acceptable and make clear your commitment to building a high-performing team. (You may find that the individual realizes that it is time to move on and this will open up the discussion about how to make that happen.)
- Next, ask a few other trusted colleagues what they think; ask whether they believe the leader you are assessing can ever be exceptional—not whether he or she can be okay, but whether he or she can help lead the team to a higher level of performance.
  - You will likely find that these colleagues not only think you should take action but they will ask why it took you so long to make the decision.
- Finally, force yourself to make a decision—yes or no. Do not let that decision be influenced by the affected leader's personal situation or whether the timing is right to make the decision.
  - Just decide whether this is the best leader to help the team to achieve success or whether you have an obligation to replace the individual

in order to do the right thing for the team and the company. If you decide not to make a change, then be certain that your decision is based on a belief that this is the best leader you can possibly find for the role and not simply unwillingness to make the tough call.

If you decide to make a change, do it fast. Get the right severance package together to make sure the person has the opportunity to move on in a positive way, then sit down with the individual and lay out your decision. Do not debate the facts of the case, but rather simply say that you have made a really tough decision that the company needs new leadership in order to succeed in the future and that you are asking the individual to move on. Then focus on how you are going to help the outgoing leader find a new opportunity and how the package you are providing will help, as well.

If the individual tries to debate his performance with you or sell you on how he is about to turn the business around, stop the conversation immediately by saying, "The decision is made, and it is not going to change. Let's focus on how we can help you make a successful transition out of the company." I know this sounds insensitive, but it is essential. You cannot waver on the decision. There is a reason you made it (because the leader in question was not delivering), and you need to follow through on it. Once you do, you will find that the change is energizing and exciting. You will have created a great opportunity to elevate or hire new talent with new ideas, but the process of getting there can be difficult.

This is part of being a senior leader. It is not a particularly fun part of the job, but it is an essential part of the job. If you cannot make the tough calls on people, then your career will most likely stall out at the director or VP level, because you cannot be successful over time without a really strong team. The farther you advance in your career, the more you will have to delegate to your team and the more you will become dependent on the strength of your team to drive success.

This is a natural part of the career-development process. In a senior leadership position, you have to trust your team and allow it to take the reins and shine. You also have to hold the team accountable for performance and be willing to make the tough decisions when team members fail to perform. It would be great if every person we hired or managed was a superstar performer, but that is not reality. In the real world, you will have to make tough decisions to continuously upgrade the team and reinvigorate the company. You may not want to do it, but you have an obligation to your team and the company not to compromise and not to hesitate.

CHAPTER 15

The Worst Part of the Job

Nobody tells you how to fire someone. It seems like an obvious thing to train people on, but I have never seen a handbook or received any training on how to let someone go effectively. I assume that this is true for most leaders; they have most likely learned through experience rather than formal coaching or instruction. But the one thing I am sure is true is that every senior leader has had to fire a number of people during his or her career. It is not a fun part of the job, but it is a necessary part of the job that we should all be prepared for.

I have never personally been fired. I probably should have been fired from one of my early jobs, but I never had to live through that experience. Although, when I think hard about it, I was effectively fired as a partner at McKinsey.

As I approached my director-election window (about eighteen months prior), my key client situations fell apart or went dormant, and I vividly remember my partner feedback that year. Basically, I was told to rebuild my client platform fast or I would be asked to leave the firm in six to twelve months. Then I was asked to compose a letter to the review committee explaining how I was going to accomplish that rebuilding.

Although it was not a surprise (I was well aware of my client situation), it still evoked strong feelings of disappointment and failure that I had somehow let down myself, along with my partners. It also evoked anger—a momentary feeling of being thrown out as soon as there was a downturn in my results.

The feelings of anger did not last long. I internalized the review and took it as a strong signal that I should move on and start looking for opportunities outside the firm. To be honest, I had already started that process, as I had already come to terms with the fact that I lacked the energy and enthusiasm for the work that would be required to rebuild my client base.

As luck would have it, I was fortunate enough to land an amazing role as the chief strategy officer for Kimberly-Clark, and that happened so quickly that I never actually had to write the "letter of shame" for the review committee. My anger quickly turned to excitement about a new opportunity and a dramatic change in my leadership journey.

I have had to fire quite a few people, however: many for performance-related issues; a larger number due to financial cutbacks; and a few based on improper behavior or conduct violations. Regardless of the reason, firing someone is never easy. It is a career- and life-altering event for most people, and it always seems to be a surprise to the affected person, no matter how well you may think the message, and the ultimate outcome, has been clearly communicated in advance. What seems obvious and necessary to the leader is often not so obvious to those who are affected by the decision.

I have observed a couple of common reactions that people typically exhibit once the feelings of surprise and anger pass. The most common reaction is a positive one. It is simply acceptance and ownership of the situation, followed by an intense focus on the essential priority of finding a new job.

Sometimes the positive reaction takes a little while to emerge. I recently fired a struggling sales leader who was initially shocked to hear that he was not performing, despite the fact that all of his colleagues and customers had made it clear that he was not creating value for them.

His immediate response was to debate the facts with me and try to demonstrate that I was wrong. When I refused to do that and instead focused on how I could help him make the transition to a new company as easily as possible, he left angry and hurt. Within forty-eight hours, however, he was back in my office discussing his severance benefits and asking for help with his job search.

I was happy to help and to be flexible on the timing of his exit because he demonstrated acceptance of the decision and a complete commitment to moving on in the most positive way possible.

This example highlights an amazing thing I have observed about the human spirit: most people are remarkably resilient. They take a blow to the ego, they deal with the initial feelings of hurt and anger, and then they focus on what matters most—providing for their families and finding a new opportunity that excites and energizes them.

More than 90 percent of the people I have observed through the process of being fired eventually react in this inspiringly positive way. Within a few days or weeks, they focus on finding a new role at another company, and they try to leave their former company in a reasonably positive manner.

I admire people who demonstrate this level of resilience, and almost without fail, I have watched them move on to good jobs at other companies well before their severance benefits expired.

The news media love to showcase stories of desperation, but the majority of my experience has been different. It is a testimony to a person's courage and persistence that they make this happen for themselves, that they stare into the abyss of failure, experience the intense feelings of anger and disappointment, and still find a way to regain their footing and confidence. Most begin to chart a new path to success, no matter how shocked and surprised they were by the news of their termination.

However, for some people, this process is not so smooth. In fact, it can be downright painful. In one of my first large leadership roles, I had to release a technical leader who was a poor communicator and a terrible people leader. Her team disliked her, and her colleagues did not trust her. Despite very direct performance feedback and coaching, she continued to struggle, and the results of her team suffered.

In my gut, I knew that firing her was going to be tough, that she would reject the decision and struggle to move on. But I owed it to her team and her colleagues to implement the decision to terminate, regardless of how much I dreaded the expected response.

I offered her a very generous severance package relative to company standards, and we were willing to offer more if we could reach a speedy and friendly agreement. In addition, I promised to help her find a new role at another company. But she was simply not capable of moving on.

The anger and feelings of betrayal this person felt were overwhelming for her. Despite evidence to the contrary, she believed that she was a strong performer who was being mistreated, and she could not let those feelings go. She hired a lawyer and sued, and the process turned ugly from there.

In the end, the legal process took three years to resolve and yielded her very little incremental benefit once the lawyers took their cut. But the three years of anger and accusations, of reliving and explaining the past, were completely paralyzing for her. Those years were effectively lost. Any chance to move on and find a new opportunity was lost as well.

For this person, suing was not just about the money; it became a matter of justice. It was her chance to prove that she was right and our assessment of her was wrong and unfair. But who really paid the price for this painful and hurtful process? She did. The company paid a few legal bills and a slightly higher settlement in the end, but other than that, it moved forward.

She stared into the abyss of failure and got lost in it. Instead of moving on and focusing on building a new future for herself at a new company, she let herself become consumed by a battle about the past, defending her past record of performance and her recollection of our past treatment of her. Most of the time, filing a lawsuit is a battle that cannot be completely won. Even a technical win often yields very little value.

I genuinely feel for people like that employee. The lingering sense of anger they feel must be debilitating.

They let themselves get caught in a fight to prove once and for all that the failure they endured was not their own, that someone else was at fault. But why?

What do they win even if they win the suit? If a leader or a company criticized your performance to the point that the decision was made to fire you and offer you a severance package, why would you invest your energy in a prolonged battle to prove them wrong? The managers have made their decision, and it is not going to change. Why would you fight that decision in an attempt to be part of a team that does not want you?

My experience is that debating and reliving the past is of very little value once the decision to fire is made. But for some people, there can be no acceptance of reality and no pivot toward the future that might allow them to focus on finding a better opportunity elsewhere.

In the course of your career, you may get fired, and you will likely have to fire someone else. Neither experience will be fun. No matter which side of the table you are on, you will either feel or witness the feelings of hurt, disappointment, and anger that accompany the event. Most of the time, those feelings will pass quickly, and you will experience a remarkable and inspiring aspect of the human spirit, the ability to rebound and refocus on what matters most.

There will also be situations where the outcome will be much less inspirational, and the experience will be disheartening. The fact that both outcomes are possible is what makes the decision to fire a tough one. It is a decision that should be taken very seriously, but it should never be avoided if it is the right thing to do for the team and the organization.

If you face the decision to terminate someone in your role, having determined that it is necessary to keep the team and the organization moving forward, remember that this is a challenging human experience. There will be intense feelings of disappointment and failure, as well as fear about what the future will bring. These are natural and powerful human emotions, and they will typically result in an angry and defensive response. But this initial response typically passes, and most people will impress you with their resilience.

Recently, I had to fire a terrific leader for cause. He was a senior leader who was driving really important change at the company, but his past involvement in activity that represented a violation of the code of conduct had come to light, and termination was the only alternative. It was a very difficult discussion, because he was otherwise a tremendous leader who was adding value to the company, and yet he needed to move on.

I did not debate the facts of the case with him because the decision was final and there was no reason to do so. I simply delivered the message in a very blunt and clear way, and then I listened to his thoughts and concerns. Finally, I spent the next hour or so trying to help him turn his attention toward finding a new future at another company.

I knew this leader was going to be successful again, if he could find a way to move on and focus on the future, so I invested my time with him trying to encourage him to do just that.

Most people will amaze and inspire you in this difficult moment. They will quickly leave the anger and disappointment behind, and they will move on and move forward, because that is what life (and necessity) demands of them. As a result, your goal as the leader accountable for firing them is to help them make this pivot toward the future as quickly as possible. Here are some guidelines:

- Be direct and to the point.
- Be fair and supportive in your offer and dealings with the individual as long as he or she responds in a rational way.
- Refuse to debate the facts of the case. Just tell the individual that the decision is made and your reason why, and then move on with planning the transition.
- Make sure the individual is absolutely clear that the decision is final and that he or she needs to turn full attention toward finding a new opportunity. If you leave an individual with hope that the decision will change, you are simply delaying the inevitable, and you are diverting the person's focus away from looking for a new role and opportunity. This is a huge mistake, as it creates false hopes that are simply a distraction from the reality of the change that must be made.
- Finally, I encourage you to be empathetic but absolutely unwavering in your resolve. Be a supportive coach who helps the individual think about the future, but never revisit the decision.

If you handle the situation in this manner, 90 to 95 percent of the people you deal with will respond in a rational manner within a few days, and they will manage the exit process professionally. Unfortunately, a small percentage of people will be unable to let go of the feelings of disappointment, failure, and anger, and those situations will be heartbreaking for everyone involved. I hope you have as few of those experiences as possible.

If you are the one getting fired, my suggestion is the same: move on and move forward. Let your feelings about the situation pass as quickly as you can; negotiate the best agreement you can with your former employer; conclude your work properly and leave in a positive way; and focus intensely on finding a new opportunity for yourself someplace else.

In addition, I would not be shy about leveraging friends at a time like this. You may feel embarrassed by the situation and be reluctant to reach out, but true friends will be happy to help connect you with new opportunities and people.

In the end, the best advice I can give anyone in this situation is to keep moving forward. Whether you have to make the tough decision to fire or live with the decision, you need to move forward and focus on the future because the future can still be shaped by your actions; the past cannot.

CHAPTER 16

Be a Coach, Not a Critic

Some leaders love to criticize. They seem to thrive on finding fault with the work of others and then correcting those mistakes. People like this have a natural talent for finding errors in anything they review. Whether it is a letter, a presentation, a strategy, or simply an idea, they can identify the mistakes and point them out.

This can be an important skill to have on your team, because it may help you identify problems early and allow you to make the final product better. You may find it hard to listen intently to people like this because criticism can suck the energy out of the room; but if you can learn to listen for the gold, the critic typically can help you improve your final work product.

However, working for a manager like this can be genuinely disheartening. When you work for someone who is always criticizing and finding fault with your work, the manner of the criticism can take away your passion and energy. In the worst cases, it may feel as though more effort is invested in finding errors than in debating good ideas and getting the best answers for the company. I am sure we all have a story or two we could tell about a boss like this. I have worked for this type of leader on a few occasions during my career, and in each case, I hated the experience.

I remember when I was an associate principal with McKinsey, working hard to prove myself at the firm. I worked with a partner on a project for a mid-sized grocery retailer who was the ultimate critic. She was a smart woman who was very good at dissecting client problems, but she completely lacked the inspirational leadership gene. She was an experienced interrogator, and she tore into analyses and presentations with a vengeance, questioning everything. Drafts of client presentations would come back covered in red ink from the hundreds of edits. In addition, every analysis and conclusion was dissected with great rigor. She was a natural critic, and she was very good at it.

Her criticism was helpful to an extent. We had a fairly young team, and I was new to the firm, so we needed her to set the bar on analytical rigor and disciplined presentation structure. But she was never able to step back from the role of the critic and think about how to get the most out of the team, or, in other words, to think like a coach. As a result, her leadership impact was effectively distilled into a never-ending series of critiques of the team's work. It was a criticism of the strategic thinking, of the analysis, or of the presentation, and what was missing was any sort of real bonding and aligning with the team around a common goal or objective. She was not really on the team or the leader of the team; she was a quality-control inspector with authority.

Leaders like this drive a team by intellectually bullying them. They tear apart the work and create an environment where people live in fear of the review process. Leaders who use such an approach will definitely drive a team to work hard and pay attention to details, but they miss out on something in the process. They fail to gain real trust and commitment from others, because they never put themselves on the same side of the table as the people they are leading.

If these critical leaders would just put down the red pen for some of their meetings and engage in an open discussion with the team members, it would completely change the leadership dynamic they create. This would allow them to openly problem-solve with their teams on issues like:

- What is the big problem we are trying to solve together?
- What are the biggest ideas we have heard or developed on how to transform the business?
- What would it take to make those ideas possible?
- How would we go about driving that change if we ran the company?
- How can we work together better as a team to drive the best outcome?

Asking a few simple questions like these and then taking the time to listen to the team can make a huge difference in terms of building trust and camaraderie. It allows the team to get its ideas on the table without the pressure of the intense review, and it allows the leader to reinforce the big-picture story about why this is important work and how it will make a difference for the company. Without this give and take, the critic simply becomes an intellectual bully, and meeting and working with him or her becomes a grind.

There were many leaders like this in consulting. I think

the training and development process at these firms tends to breed a higher percentage of people with this critical style. In addition, the constant stream of PowerPoint presentations, which are produced for clients, makes an easy target for a critical leader. But this leadership trait is by no means limited to consulting. I have seen many leaders throughout my career whose first inclination is to grab a red pen and start editing (criticizing).

I remember one leader I worked for who had transitioned into a large operating role and who seemed to think only in terms of analyses and presentations. I never once saw him have an open discussion with his team. He would ask for presentations on every topic and then he would grab a pen and dig in. In many cases, he would not even look at the person presenting; he would stare down at the presentation and then question or challenge the thinking and wording. It was almost as if the ideas did not count if they were not captured appropriately in the document.

Imagine the relationships this leader developed (or failed to develop) with his team members. He would call them to his office to discuss an issue, ask them to prepare a presentation in advance, and then, when they got to his office, he would sit in judgment, behind his desk with his pen, tearing apart the document and only looking up once in a while to ask a question.

This is not a recipe for strong relationship building, and not surprisingly, his team members felt very distant from him. We all were ready to be interrogated when our turn came, but we never felt like we were really on his team; instead we felt browbeaten and disengaged. He slowly wore us down until we were desperate to move on to any other role we could. Not surprisingly, he got terrible upward feedback in terms of his people leadership skills.

Don't get me wrong—critical thinking is an essential skill for a leader. Executives need to be able to break apart an issue, challenge their teams to think critically about how to solve the problem, and then work with them to develop a detailed plan of attack. But editing a document and finding analytical or grammatical errors is not leadership, nor is it the primary goal of leadership. The goal is to problem-solve with the team, to get them to understand the challenges and opportunities, to listen to their ideas and inspire them to think big about the differences they can make, and then align on a plan the entire team can support.

Success generally requires that a leader take ownership and lead the implementation of a plan. Leaders who focus solely on indulging their penchant for criticism never really partner with their teams. They do not engage the team's imagination and creativity, but rather they simply critique the work of the team members and send them on their way (devoid of energy and dreading the next review meeting).

I have made this mistake myself over the years. I remember being in my first leadership role at NutraSweet, a strategy role, and how my first inclination was to jump into editing mode. We would put together an analysis of a key strategic decision for senior management, and my team would look to me to make sure the presentation made sense. Since I had practice at presentations from my consulting background, I jumped right in. I would grab the pen and start editing the document. It was an automatic reaction.

As I look back now, I think about a better approach.

I would likely start in a completely different manner. I would kick off the discussion by asking some questions: what is the problem we are trying to solve; why does it make a difference to the company; what are the big risks the leadership team should consider before making the decision; what is the upside opportunity for the company; and what will it take to implement the decision?

This approach would likely lead to a fifteen-minute discussion with the team that would allow us to align on the priorities, clarify our thinking on what matters most, explore some big ideas and issues together, and focus the presentation on the issues and information senior leadership would need to make the best decision for the company. More importantly, it would allow the team to problem-solve with me in a collaborative way because it would provide space and time for them to contribute and give me a chance to listen and learn from their ideas.

This is the core of the issue: there is no doubt that leaders should aspire to being rigorous and demanding, because leaders with these traits challenge the team to deliver higher quality work and raise the bar on performance. It is important to set high expectations on analytical rigor and the quality of staff work. But you have to be more than just critical and demanding. Your goal as a leader should be to get the most out of your people—to listen and learn from them, and to elevate and inspire the team to own the strategy and be willing to take the actions necessary to bring it to life. You will not get there by simply grabbing a red pen and tearing apart their documents or work.

If you are one who tends to jump right into editing

your teams' work (as I can be at times), try the following techniques to be a better coach for your team:

- First off, never start with a pen in your hand. In fact, do not even start by paging through the document. Start the conversation by asking the team why this matters, what the opportunity is, what their concerns are, and what it will take to succeed.
- Next, take the time to listen to the team for a few minutes. Let them talk about the work they are doing, what worries or excites them, and what they hope to get out of this meeting (and what decisions or support they need from you).
- Once you have had the chance to talk with the team and hear their ideas, then you can ask them to take you through the key pages in the document or presentation that highlight the key issues and ideas and the team's recommendation.
- Then you can really dig into the recommendation and the logic behind it. Why does the team support the idea? Is their logic sound? Have they completed the right analysis to get to the best answer? Have they thought through what it will take to implement the decision and the likely repercussions?
- After all of this, you can help the team members tell their story in a more compelling way by giving them feedback on how to organize the storyline and the presentation in a manner that will engage people and drive action.
- Finally, never forget to ask the team members what they need from you in order to implement the

decision and deliver results. This question allows the team to see you as a partner and collaborator rather than just a boss.

Imagine how working this way with your team would change the relationship dynamic. Instead of teams fearing the review process, they would look forward to the opportunity to problem-solve with you and get your coaching on how to make their work better. This approach may seem like it will take more time when you are already rushed and busy; however, my experience is that such meetings will actually go faster because you get the big issues on the table up front and focus the discussion on what really matters, rather than doing a forced walk through a document.

I seldom have a one-hour meeting that lasts the full hour because the process of stepping back and engaging in an open discussion with the team allows us to quickly build trust and to focus on the key priorities. I have heard this referred to as the "speed of trust," and I have learned to believe in it over time.

In my view, we should all aspire to have this type of relationship with our teams. The people who work for us are the lifeblood of every company. They write the marketing plans, solve the big operational issues, manage the important customer relationships, and develop the new products. Their work drives the business forward day in and day out.

Our job as leaders is to empower, energize, and focus these teams so that they can execute their work faster and more effectively, thus making a bigger impact on the business. It is through them that our work becomes meaningful. We do not win or succeed when they leave our offices exhausted and browbeaten following another meeting full of criticism. We win when they are motivated, focused, and ready to implement the actions required to deliver on the strategies we have developed with them. So next time you sit down with your team, drop the pen and think about being a coach, not a critic. I guarantee that it will fundamentally change your relationship with your team.

CHAPTER 17

Sharing the Stage

Last year, I happened to see a video of Billy Joel sharing his experiences (and his music) with students at Vanderbilt University. During the course of the presentation, a student by the name of Michael Pollack bravely stood up and asked if he could come on stage and play the song "New York State of Mind" with Joel. Incredibly, Joel paused for just a moment and then said, "Okay," and the aspiring artist ran up on stage and absolutely blew the room away with his performance.

Joel's reaction made a big impression on me. Here was a superstar performer, up on stage sharing his lifetime of experiences and success, and he is confident enough to let a brash young pianist come up and steal the show. He could have politely rejected the student's request and nobody would have thought negatively about it, but he didn't. Instead he shared the stage with an unknown artist, and in the course of those few minutes, he probably launched a career. Joel was self-confident, he was generous, and he was a leader, because great leaders do this for talented young leaders.

I immediately penned a note to my team and asked them to watch the video and think about whom they have invited up on stage recently. I believe that sharing the stage is a terrific leadership lesson.

Throughout my career, leaders have been willing to bet on me. Despite my flaws and immaturity, they saw potential in me, and they went out of their way to help me realize my potential. The first leader to really take a risk on me was the VP of finance at NutraSweet. He had worked with me at Boston Consulting Group, so he knew both my strengths and my weaknesses. Despite the risks, he was willing to entrust a twenty-four-year-old with an important leadership role on his team. He saw strong problem-solving capability and nascent leadership skills in me and obviously believed that the potential upside was greater than the downside risk of hiring an immature young leader with a penchant for brash comments and rash decisions in the heat of the moment.

This kind of risk-taking is the reality of sharing the stage and betting on someone: it is seldom a guaranteed decision. When you trust people to step up into bigger leadership roles, they are never perfect for the role (nobody is); they are never fully ready; and there is inevitably some risk that they will fail (or at least struggle) in their new positions. But confident leaders courageously make the decision to bet on talent, challenge talented team members with big new positions, and shine a light on them so that they can be noticed by other leaders in the organization.

The next person to place a big bet on me was the founder at Whitlock Packaging Corporation. Although we had many differences and parted under less-than-perfect terms, I give him credit for taking an enormous risk to bring new talent and new energy to his company. Put yourself in his shoes for a minute: imagine that you are hiring a new president to run the company you founded, which now has more than a thousand employees and three manufacturing plants, and you pick a thirty-four-year-old with only a few years of real operating/profit-and-loss experience. He had to know that there would be mistakes made and some growing pains as I stepped into this big new leadership role, but he made the decision to bet on me, and he was willing to let me run the company with minimal oversight.

As I think back on this today, I realize the courage it took for him to make that decision. He was handing over his company to an unproven leader because he believed it would bring new ideas and important changes to the business. All senior leaders will face this decision at some point in their careers. They will have talent on their team that they want to develop and grow. They will appreciate the fresh insights and energy of those team members, and at some point they will have to promote that talent beyond their experience in order to understand their full potential. It can be a troubling decision, and it takes courage and confidence to make it; however, those bets are really important because if you get it right, you can change the future trajectory of a company.

After I left Whitlock, when I was struggling in my first year back in consulting at McKinsey in Charlotte, there were a few additional leaders at the firm who bet on me. One of the leaders of the operations practice at the firm and the head of the southern office both invested to help me build a successful program, which allowed me to find my leadership niche in the firm. That niche was at the intersection of the operations practice and the consumer practice. They provided coaching, connected me with client situations, helped me develop and commercialize client service materials, and generally helped me define my unique leadership platform at McKinsey. Without their investment in me, I am not sure I would have made it through the partner-election process.

There were many people they could have invested their time in; the firm was full of terrific talent, but they chose to invest in me because they saw experience and leadership skills that would add value to the firm. They believed that I would add value to the organization as a mentor and coach for talent in both the southern region and the operations practice.

This highlights another learning for me, which is that leaders have to prioritize which team members they invest in. You will have to choose because your time is not limitless, and the decision should be based on what you feel is missing from your team and organization. When you recognize leadership and skill gaps in your team, part of your job will be to find people who possess those capabilities and invest disproportionately in them in order to grow those leaders into larger leadership roles that can help you shape the organization for the future. This takes wisdom and vision, as well as real insight into your team and what they need to grow and succeed.

Another leader who bet big on me was the CEO of Kimberly-Clark. He bet on me three separate times. The first time was when he hired me into the chief strategy officer role. From our first two-hour meeting, he must have realized that I was a very aggressive and high-energy leader who would step on some toes (and break a few things) in a conservative organization like Kimberly-Clark. But he took a risk and hired me anyway because he believed that his organization needed that spark to continue to grow and develop new skills.

After just a few years in the strategy role, he bet on me again, trusting me to lead the $3.5 billion Kimberly-Clark Professional (KCP) business. It was the biggest operating role I had ever been given, and he had to be a little nervous during those first six months when we struggled to turn around the business. I know I was. But he made the call and supported me in the role, and it was an unbelievable leadership experience that transformed me as a leader and gave the team the opportunity to transform the strategy and trajectory of the business as well.

After I had been just twenty months in the KCP role, the CEO bet on me one more time when he asked me to take the position of president, Kimberly-Clark International. It was a huge role, leading the fastest-growing part of the company that was essential to our long-term success and the valuation of the company. I had never run a business so large, and once again, he had to be worried that my hyper-aggressive style could cause some disruption in this key business segment for KC. However, he decided to bet on me regardless of these concerns, and he gave me the freedom to lead the team, as well as the support I needed to make key decisions and drive change.

The key learning for me is simply that strong leaders are courageous enough, insightful enough, and visionary enough to pick high-potential talent to invest in; challenge those people with big roles that stretch their abilities; and support those leaders through the inevitable ups and downs that come with growth and development. These are not easy decisions to make, but they are essential to the success of a leader and the health of an organization over time.

I am sure that all successful senior leaders have bet on a number of young leaders during the course of their careers. A few probably failed, but many more succeeded, and those who succeeded helped take their companies to the next level of performance.

Today, this learning is central to how I view my role as a senior executive. I know that I will need to hire talent, promote talent, and develop talent that will shape the organization. I will need to push them into roles that will stretch their abilities, and when the time is right, I will need to step aside so that the best of that talent can take my job and lead the company to an even better future. I think that every senior leader should be thinking this way, and they should be practicing this as part of their leadership routines. Senior leaders should ask themselves the following questions:

1) **Have I picked out four or five up-and-coming leaders who could rise to the top of the company?** In my view, leaders have to be decisive and select a set of people to invest in disproportionately. They should make it known to the rest of the senior team that they have decided to invest in those leaders, and they should force an active dialogue with that team about these young leaders every six months, so that they can actively manage their career paths and help them get the right experiences to be successful long-term.

2) **Am I actively betting on the high-potentials?** It is one thing to know who they are, but it takes courage to actually bet on the best talent and

invest personally to help them succeed. Great leaders need to hold themselves accountable for truly "betting" on great talent, which means promoting them into roles that are beyond their comfort zones and that involve some risk, and then they need to be available as coaches when those young leaders inevitably struggle with their expanded responsibilities.

3) **Am I willing to create the opportunities for those leaders to grow?** The best positions and opportunities for development may not be available when the high-potential candidates are ready. When that is the case, courageous leaders need to take action and be willing to move leaders out in order to nurture the next generation of talent. This is a very tough job because the incumbent leaders affected by these moves may be trusted colleagues, but it is essential to maintain the development trajectory of the most talented future leaders, as well as to keep the organization fresh and energized with new ideas.

4) **Am I willing to move aside when the time comes?** This is the toughest decision by far. Many successful CEOs have failed to move aside when the time was right for the next generation to take over. It is a very hard decision that is made even more difficult by boards that are naturally conservative and would prefer stability versus change. Another factor in a public company is the investors and analysts, who often jump on any change as a sign of trouble. But great leaders know when to step aside and allow the next generation to take the

reins so that the organization can continue to move forward. I think this may be the toughest job of a CEO, and I am sure that many fail at it.

I try to ask these questions of myself and my team on a consistent basis. As a team, we need to be clear which people we are investing in and why. More important, we need to be willing to take action, betting on the best talent by providing them with stretch roles and challenging assignments and coaching them as they learn and develop as leaders. This is not an exact science, but senior leaders need to hold themselves accountable for developing the next generation of leaders. Leaders need to be courageous enough to bet on the next generation, and they need to be sufficiently self-aware and self-confident that they can step aside when the time is right.

There is no specific method to determining when it is time for a leader to step aside, but I think the best barometer may be found in the boldness of their vision for change. When senior leaders are first promoted into big leadership roles, they inevitably come in with ideas to transform the business and make it fundamentally better. Often, they have been hungry to make changes for some time, but they have been unable to act until that moment. That vision for change drives action and moves the organization forward in a fast-changing world.

When those big ideas run out and a leader is simply managing incremental improvements in the business, then it is probably time to move on. The time it will take for this to happen will vary dramatically based upon the individual and his or her level of interest and passion for the business. But once those bold ideas run out, once the vision for what comes next looks more and more like a marginal improvement over what the company is already doing today, that is the moment when every leader must think hard about clearing the way for someone with a bigger appetite for change and the energy to make it happen. That is a lot to ask of any person, but it is probably the most important decision a leader will make in his or her career.

CHAPTER 18

Piercing the Bubble

As you get more senior in your career, some interesting changes will begin to happen around you. The most obvious is that you make a lot more money, and this allows you to purchase a nice house, own nicer cars, belong to private clubs, pay people to take care of your house/yard/kids/pets/etc., and enjoy nice dinners out and exciting vacations with your friends and family. It will surprise you how suddenly you can afford things that were only a dream early in your career.

Things will change in your work life as well. You will probably have a private secretary who will take care of virtually all tedious administrative tasks for you and closely schedule your time, controlling who has access to you. In addition, you will likely begin flying first class (or in a private jet), stay in the best hotels, and be catered to when you visit local teams. You will do less of the real work and spend more of your time reviewing the work of others and providing feedback.

In addition to all of this, you will find that the relationship dynamics with your teams may change. They may be more reserved and cautious in terms of what they share with you and what they choose not to disclose, and they may be nervous prior to a meeting with you. Even worse, they might be reluctant to disagree with you in a meeting, given your position in the company and the perceived risk to their careers. Stranger still is the fact that your ideas will suddenly be better (at least that is what you will hear from the team), and your jokes will suddenly be funnier.

Any one of these changes in isolation may not affect your view of the world or your daily life much, but in combination they can fundamentally change things. With little advance notice, you will find that a bubble begins to form around you as a senior leader, a bubble that has the potential to separate you from the real world. The bubble will be almost unnoticeable at first; it will likely get lost in the excitement of a big new role and the challenges that come with that promotion. But if you take the time to reflect, you will suddenly recognize that you are becoming more and more disconnected from the daily life of your consumers, customers, and employees, and this can be a dangerous phenomenon.

I first noticed the bubble about six months into my job as president of the international division for Kimberly-Clark. After the promotion, I moved back to Dallas from Atlanta, and I did exactly what you might expect:

- I purchased a beautiful house in an affluent neighborhood just north of town.
- I joined a private country club where a number of other senior executives were members.
- I purchased more exotic cars.
- I had a private secretary who was extremely efficient, and she quickly took over many of my personal affairs as well as my business support needs.

- My social circle began to narrow as I was more cautious about those with whom I spent time outside of work.
- I began serving on a public company board of directors.
- And I suddenly had the financial means to not worry about money—ever, because our lifestyle was modest relative to my income.

These changes were subtle at first. They were a natural progression of the increasing affluence that comes with success. But I noticed other changes as well:

- I noticed that when I traveled, the trips were planned to the smallest detail; hotel rooms were always suites, and I was checked in prior to arrival.
- The daily agendas were scheduled down to the minute with speeches and meetings.
- I never had to bring money with me because everything was paid for.
- I noticed that I no longer introduced myself anymore; people introduced themselves to me. They all knew who I was prior to walking in the door of my office.
- I also noticed that people were much more prepared when they came to meet with me. They were less likely to have casual conversations and instead seemed to always come to meetings with a detailed PowerPoint document and a decision they wanted me to make.
- Finally, I noticed that I had less time available to openly problem-solve ideas; my calendar was

getting booked up farther and farther in advance, and it was harder for people to connect with me.

These changes happened almost imperceptibly, but I pretty quickly realized that in combination, they were troublesome. In total, these changes created a chasm between me and the people I needed to serve: our customers, employees, and stakeholders. I found myself becoming more and more disconnected from the organization and from the marketplace, and I worried about it.

To pierce the bubble that was forming around me, I began to implement a few simple practices designed to decrease the distance between me and the people who worked close to the front lines of our dispersed global organization. None of these are breakthrough ideas, but as a whole, they helped break down the barriers I could feel forming around me.

First off, I began to adjust my travel plans to create substantial unplanned time to sit down and talk at length with frontline leaders, top talent, and senior regional executives whenever I visited a market or regional office. In addition, I encouraged teams to finish all presentation materials in fifteen to twenty minutes so that we could spend the rest of the time talking about their ideas and what I could do to help them be successful.

I also began blocking substantial free time on my calendar for casual/ad hoc discussions, so that people could stop by and talk about pressing issues and problem-solve their plans with me in a more relaxed and free-flowing manner. Finally, I began scheduling at least one call every week with a frontline leader somewhere around the world. In these calls, I would just listen to their challenges, ask questions about their business, and let them ask questions of me. These calls turned out to be incredibly informative for me and very inspirational to the local leaders who invested their time to share insights with me.

I am sure I will need to develop and implement additional ideas and practices to maintain the connection with all levels of the organization. The problem is not going away, so I have to work at addressing it continuously. I have watched other leaders fail to work at this challenge and end up completely disconnected from reality. I recall working with one senior executive who was unexpectedly promoted to the CEO role late in his career, and I could not believe how arrogant and detached he seemed to be within twelve months of assuming that role.

Prior to his elevation to the CEO position, he could be arrogant at times, but he was generally a down-to-earth person who was easy to talk to and work with. But within a year of becoming CEO, he was incorrigible. He became increasingly opinionated and directive; his listening skills diminished dramatically; and he quickly seemed out of touch with the world around him.

But imagine the environment he must live in every day as CEO of a large company. He flies only on private jets; his teams plan every trip and cater to his every need; he has an eight-figure income that is beyond conception for most people; and very few people are courageous enough to disagree or debate with him. He has a massive bubble surrounding him that has made him detached, arrogant, and unfortunately, a less-likeable person.

As you progress in your career, these changes are likely to affect you as well. It will probably begin when you reach the senior director or vice president level at a company (or partner level at a consulting or law firm), and with each level you attain from that point, the bubble will become more substantial and more dangerous. All of a sudden, you will be surrounded by new possessions you never thought you would have and new people who are increasingly eager to please you. Your office will be bigger; your assistant will take care of more of your administrative and personal tasks; your calendar will become booked farther and farther in advance; you will spend less time with customers, consumers, and frontline employees; and, if you are aware, you will begin to notice the bubble forming around you.

It is not your fault; these are natural changes that come with the achievement of more senior positions in an organization, but you are accountable for piercing the bubble if you want to stay connected with the organization and the marketplace.

My first suggestion is simply to be aware—look around you and try to notice the bubble. Ask yourself how connected you are with all levels of the organization, how much time you spend working with and learning from frontline managers and from the marketplace, how much real problem-solving time you are investing with your teams. If the answer to these questions is "not much," then you have a problem to solve. It is not a difficult problem to solve, but you need to be aware that the problem exists, and you have to have the desire to address it.

Although I am sure there are plenty of senior leaders who really do not care much about piercing the bubble, if you have the desire to change the situation, then I would suggest a few simple steps:

- Consider booking four to six hours of free time into your calendar each week to allow for ad hoc problem solving with other leaders.
- Try to call at least one frontline leader or worker each week and learn about his or her reality and what the business looks like from the ground level.
- When you travel to local markets, try to travel by yourself on some occasions, and consider visiting a few local customers with a first-level sales person.
- In addition, try to do fewer speeches when you visit local operations and spend more time talking with top talent and local leaders, seeking to learn about their reality.
- When you meet with teams to review analyses and proposals, try to make the meetings less formal. Ask the teams to shorten the formal component of the presentation and spend time problem-solving with them in more of a peer-to-peer environment
- Consider asking a young leader (someone who has been out of college for less than seven or eight years) to be a reverse mentor, and create an environment where that leader can provide real feedback about what it is like to work far down in the organization.

These are just a few ideas; I am sure there are better ones that you can find or come up with. There are many potential techniques. The key ingredient is the desire to pierce the bubble. I am sure that there are a number of executives who see all of these ideas as silly and a waste of time. They do not see the issue and therefore the entire concept of piercing the bubble seems ridiculous. But trust me, I have seen far too many executives become isolated from their teams, their customers, and the marketplace—and the results can be horrific.

I will not bother listing all of the examples of companies that lost their way and lost relevance in a fast-changing marketplace and eventually disappeared, but the threat is real. So, if you have the chance to create a better future for your company and the desire to stay connected so that you can continue to add value and drive positive change, then grab hold of that opportunity and be willing to actively pierce the bubble that is probably forming around you. It will make you a better leader; it will inspire your team; and it may have a huge impact on the long-term health of the business you lead.

CHAPTER 19

An Evolving Lens

After many years, many inspiring successes, and an equal number of disappointing failures (only a few of which I have shared in this book), I have developed a lens on leadership that serves as a trusted guide in my career and life. It is a constantly evolving lens, as life's lessons never really stop and neither does my learning journey. But I have developed a few benchmarks and metrics that I use to evaluate how I am doing on my journey. These criteria work well in helping me evaluate other leaders as well.

I will not claim that my list is unique (or exhaustive); in fact, I am sure you have heard most of these ideas before. But they serve as a great tool to self-assess my performance and understand where I might be falling below my aspirations as a leader. I do not strive for perfection against all of these criteria, but I try to identify the two or three on which I can improve the most, and then I consciously work on those with my team. I hope you find a few of them helpful on your leadership journey.

1) **Develop a compelling vision** or "big *why*" for your business or function. It is very hard to motivate a team and drive meaningful change if you cannot

articulate a vision that matters to the customer and to your team. This vision cannot be just a number, a sales or profit-increase target. It must be something your organization will do for customers that is both unique and valued. Your vision should inspire. It should describe why your team matters, the difference they make for the business or the customer, and why people should care.

I have learned that most teams typically will not care much about making more money or gaining a little more market share, so you need to work with the team to describe its unique value and point of difference in a manner that captures team members' hearts as well as their minds. I am constantly asking myself *why* do we matter, *why* are we different or better, *why* do customers care, *why* will they continue to buy from us, and *why* should my team care about serving them? If I cannot answer these questions, then we probably lack a compelling vision and mission for our business.

2) **Focus on a pragmatic and simple plan.** The operating plan for your business or function has to be simple, no more than four or five priorities on which your team stays relentlessly focused. You can probably articulate ten or fifteen things the team could work on, but I guarantee you that more than 80 percent of the value will be delivered by the top four or five ideas. A long list of priorities will simply distract and fragment the effort of your team.

Transformational leaders work with the team

to determine the top four or five key actions and initiatives that really matter, and then they focus the team on delivering against those critical goals. They focus on metrics that make progress against these goals visible. They make sure those key initiatives are fully resourced and supported with top talent. And they personally lean in and follow up on those critical priorities to ensure progress. This level of discipline and focus is required to drive consistent progress and help the working teams quickly overcome the inevitable barriers that will emerge.

3) **Establish stretch goals and aspirations.** In my experience, incremental improvement goals drive incremental thinking. Without something to inspire and challenge their thinking, people tend to rely on the same ideas and approaches they have always used and simply push a little harder than the previous year. If you want people to think big and try new ideas, you need to challenge them with goals that are impossible to achieve without innovation.

It is important to distinguish between commitments and aspirations when using this approach. You may have to maintain budget commitments for the business that are more realistic, but you need to include some aspirational goals for key improvement objectives or initiatives in order to drive creative thinking.

I strive to set challenging goals with my team on all of our key initiatives, because every time we work against these seemingly impossible goals, the team finds a way to achieve them. It typically requires us to take some risks or invest in new ideas, but that is how organizations innovate and get stronger.

4) **Monitor performance consistently, and drive fast decision-making.** Once the most important initiatives are set, it is essential to establish a consistent performance management dialogue for the business. In my view, the old business adage that "what gets measured gets managed" could not be more true. Great teams and great leaders hold monthly or weekly performance management discussions. They look at the key metrics (not an exhaustive data set—but the most important metrics) for their business or function together. They determine what is going well and where the problems are, and they quickly lean in together to address issues.

The key is to make problems visible, focus on the biggest issues, and then drive a collaborative problem-solving dialogue with the team. At the end of these meetings, I always like to agree on the successes and accomplishments we will celebrate with our team, as well as the issues we need to focus on together and the accountability for following up on each issue. We then capture those successes and challenges in a monthly CFO letter back to the organization, so that everyone can be inspired by the successes; be aware of the issues and challenges we see as a leadership team; be clear on who is responsible for following up on the problems; and know with whom they will likely need to work to continue to drive progress.

5) **Be transparent and direct.** As a leader, you cannot waste time trying to make everybody happy. You need to have the courage and conviction to share your perspectives and opinions openly with your team. I think the best leaders find a way to do this in an optimistic or positive way, but they still share their ideas and concerns directly and in the moment with their teams. They do the same with performance feedback; they do not wait for the right time or place, and they do not sugar-coat feedback.

   The best leaders grab people right after the meeting or event, and they courageously share their ideas about how that leader could be even more effective in the future. Leading and communicating in this manner creates clarity and trust with the team. The team members understand the leader's perspective and opinion; they get to hear the reasoning and logic for those concerns in real time; and they get the chance to develop and improve from constructive feedback provided in a timely manner.

   I think it is a mistake to wait for the "perfect time" or the "perfect words" to coach an individual or a team. The most authentic and transparent approach is to simply put the issues on the table in a positive way and be direct about what will be required in order to deliver on your expectations.

6) **Make the tough calls on people.** This is the toughest job of a leader—and the most important one. The more senior you get, the more dependent you become on the quality of your team to drive

execution and deliver results. As a result, if you want to progress to the most senior levels of any organization, you must be able to recruit great people, promote great people, develop great people, and clear the way for those talented people to move up by holding every leader in the organization accountable for his or her performance.

You cannot compromise. You have to hold people to a very high leadership standard and be willing to move people out when they are not meeting that standard. I know this sounds harsh, but it is essential to the success of every leader. If you have a weak leader on your team, I guarantee you that everyone knows it. Their colleagues know it, their teams know it, and your boss knows it.

When you fail to act with courage and take action relative to that leader, you are telling the organization that you either lack the insight to see what they see or the courage to take action on the problem. Neither is a good signal to send to your organization.

Nothing is more important to your success over time than making the tough calls on people—both taking the risks you must take to promote talented leaders and making the tough decisions you will have to make to remove leaders who cannot take the team to the next level. This is a make-or-break capability for a leader. If you fail at this one, you will stall in your career.

7) **Be a coach that energizes the team.** You can choose to be a coach or you can choose to be a critic. Critics tear issues and teams apart. They

interrogate people, break the issues down, and they find the problems. It may help a team improve the quality of its work or presentation, but it is unlikely to inspire a team to higher levels of performance over time.

In my view, great coaches build the best teams and organizations. They still call out the issues and problems, and they still dig into the details, but they quickly turn the conversation to the opportunity. Coaches express the change they want in a positive way, and they help the team see the possibility that could be created if they invested energy to adjust their thinking or analysis of a given situation.

When people leave the office of a critic, they look beaten-down and tired, worn out by the intense scrutiny and criticism. When people leave the office of a good coach, they are energized and focused. They understand the problems, but they also understand the opportunity they can create if they fix the problem, and they are excited to get started making those changes a reality.

How do people look when they leave your office? If you are going to build a truly inspired team, you need to know the answer to that question and be willing to adjust your style accordingly. Great teams make great leaders successful, and critics seldom build great teams.

8) **Strive to be humble, and release your agenda.** Humility is not typically the strong suit of senior leaders; neither is listening with real energy or the desire to learn. For some reason, senior leaders seem to get so full of themselves, so confident in

their opinions and perspectives, that they stop listening and they stop seeking to learn from others. This is hubris in my view, and it has the potential to sabotage a leader. It is simply too easy to become disconnected from the realities of the business, disconnected from customers and consumers, disconnected from the people who actually do the value-added work in a company, and disconnected from the realities of competing in a fast-changing marketplace.

I have watched leaders become so arrogant that they simply walk into every meeting and tell the team what to do. They do not listen to the team's ideas or seek to challenge their thinking. They simply mandate the direction or answer to the team and expect them to execute it. This is a dangerous approach in my opinion, because the business world is changing so fast today that you need to constantly introduce new ideas and thinking into your own, in order to stay current and fresh.

As a result, the best leaders enter every meeting looking to learn. The best leaders release their own agendas, and they ask their teams to share important insights into customer and consumer behavior. They ask about competitive trends and activity, and they ask for the team's recommendation and reasoning. By taking a moment to suspend their own egos and agendas and investing just a little time up front to ask a few key questions, they create a learning environment.

The result is a culture in which the team

knows its ideas will be valued, and the leader has the opportunity to learn and benefit from those ideas. This is the kind of leader I would like to be. I am sure I do not live up to this in every interaction with my team, but I hope and strive to.

9) **Show up with passion and energy every day.** I have a saying I use with my team, which is simply that "leaders never get to have a bad day." I realize this is an impossible standard to live up to, but I still ask them to try. My reasoning is simple: the people and teams who schedule time on our collective calendars often wait weeks or months to meet with us, share their ideas and recommendations, and gain our support and guidance for their projects or initiatives.

If we have a bad day and let it affect our leadership, the team members have a bad month, and they leave our offices disheartened and uninspired. That is a huge waste. I want every team to be focused and inspired when they leave my office because they are the people who will execute our plans and deliver the value.

I no longer get the opportunity to develop the marketing plans, run the operations, manage our supply chain, or innovate products. Teams that work for me do that. I get the chance to challenge them, coach them, and problem-solve with them, but they are the ones who lead the hard work required to bring these initiatives to life in the marketplace. If I fail to inspire them, then I fail to help us win as a team.

Great leaders are servant leaders, not dictators.

They recognize that building teams of focused and inspired people is the best path to success, and they strive to bring energy and passion to every discussion and every person so that the organization can develop and improve.

10) **Never stop learning and refuse to fall into the trap of the *do-nothing strategy*.** I think the world is changing far too fast for any leader to remain static. The minute a leader stops learning, he or she can quickly become stale and out of touch. As a result, I think the best leaders strive to build learning into everything they do. They ask their teams to provide learning about the marketplace, the consumer or customer, and the competitors. In addition, they challenge the leadership team to visit other companies to gain insights and ideas, and they try to spend time in the market with customers and consumers so that they can see the business through their eyes.

Great leaders continue to learn about their own personal strengths and weaknesses. Some might think that when you reach the top levels of a company, the performance feedback slows down or stops, but this should not be the case. There is plenty of feedback from the board, from other senior leaders, and from the organization that can be gathered and should be heard. This information provides terrific insight into how a leader is perceived and the impact he or she is having on the organization, both good and bad. Some leaders seem to assume that once they reach the top of the pyramid they no longer need to learn from this feedback (perhaps they think they have achieved perfection), but if they genuinely want their teams to win, it seems logical that they would strive to get better as leaders and increase their value as coaches for the organization.

Finally, learning leaders work hard to avoid the trap of the do-nothing strategy. They refuse to kill every new idea that comes along with paralyzing analysis versus the base case. Instead, they find low-cost ways to test new ideas that have the potential to transform the business, and they personally support a handful of experiments or innovations on a continuous basis. This allows the organization to adapt, to learn from an ever-changing world, and to discover new sources of growth for the future.

I realize that this is a "top-ten list" and that it is impossible to stay focused on this many leadership capabilities. But the goal is not to strive for perfection against every single item on the list, but rather to identify the short list on which you have the greatest opportunity to improve. For me, numbers two and eight are my biggest development opportunities. I have a tendency to develop too many ideas and fragment the team, and I have to push myself to slow down and listen to the team so that I get the benefit of their ideas. Knowing these are my biggest development opportunities, I consciously work at both of them.

In order to make sure that I do not fragment our agenda (number two), I regularly ask my team to challenge me if there is any danger of diluting the focus on our aligned plan. In addition, after we review our progress against the key business initiatives each month, I ask the team if we have too many projects and whether we should consider further narrowing our focus. I use these questions as a forcing mechanism to make sure we stay focused and that I do not derail the team by introducing too many ideas and too much complexity.

For number eight (releasing my agenda), I commit to blocking the first fifteen or twenty minutes of every meeting to just talking with the team about its biggest ideas. I ask the team members to put the PowerPoint pages aside and simply tell me their big idea, what insight they used to develop the idea, what value they believe it will create, and why they think it is a big opportunity for the company. By forcing a relaxed conversation and asking the team members to "just talk to me" about their work and their ideas, I find that I can release my agenda, and this gives me a chance to listen, learn, and think before I jump into problem-solving mode.

I would encourage you to think through the list of ten criteria above and think about your biggest improvement areas. It might be helpful to ask a couple of trusted colleagues to give you their perspectives as well. Developing self-awareness and getting feedback will allow you to narrow the list down to two or three big opportunities for you to develop and grow as a leader. Then you can begin to work on these collaboratively with your team. I recommend telling team members what you are working on and asking for their feedback. Just the simple act of stating your development goals and asking for their help and input will make an immediate impact on the team.

In the end, this all comes down to self-awareness and

self-confidence. If you are courageous enough to look at yourself objectively, and ask others to provide direct feedback, then you will begin a journey toward becoming a better leader. I realize that this can be a scary thought for some people. Some worry that others will think less of them because they have imperfections and development needs; but perfection is simply a myth that distracts us. We all have imperfections and opportunities to grow and develop as leaders. Once we accept that as a fundamental truth, we open up amazing possibilities for personal growth and development. I wish you success in uncovering those possibilities for yourself and your team.